The Ultimate Guide To Wholesaling Real Estate:

How To Find, Sign And Close Your First 100 Deals Within 90 Days.

Copyright © 2019 by Liran Koren

All Rights Reserved.

First Edition

ISBN: 9781707815029

Limit of Liability: This book is presented for informational purposes only and not as a source of professional investing, legal or tax advisement. The author does not assume any responsibility for errors, inaccuracies or omissions. Although the author has made every reasonable attempt to ensure the information contained herein is accurate and up to date, the author makes no representations or warranties regarding the accuracy or completeness of the contents of this book.

Any trademarks, product names or named features are the property of the respective owners and are used only for reference. The author makes no explicit or implicit endorsement of any product or service mentioned in this book.

Table of Contents

Common Misunderstandings About Wholesaling Real Estate 1

    What Precisely Are We Talking About By Wholesaling? How Easy Is It In Practice? 1

    If This Business Is So Competitive, What Chance Do I Have? 5

    I Don't Know If This Is Right For Me. I've Heard A Lot Of Negative Things About Wholesalers. 7

    How Much Can I Realistically Earn By Wholesaling? 9

    Is Wholesaling Legal In My State? I Don't Have A Real Estate License. 9

    I Don't Know. I Feel Uncomfortable Hunting Down People Going Through Hard Times So I Can Buy Their House Cheaply. That Just Feels Wrong. 13

Phase I – Laying The Foundation for Lasting Success 15

    The Keys To Wholesaling Like A Boss 15

        How to find distressed sellers before anyone else. 15

        How to gain that all-important negotiating leverage with sellers. 16

        How to vet your buyers as thoroughly as your sellers so you're only working with the most reliable partners. 19

        Adopting a high-volume mindset to take your game to the next level. 21

    What Makes A Legitimate Wholesale Lead? 22

    Classes Of Leads For Wholesalers 24

        Tier 1 – Hot leads 24

        Tier 2 – Warm leads 31

        Tier 3 – Wildcard leads. 36

    How Should We NOT Source Leads? 40

        Leads from cash buyer websites. 40

        Any pre-made list of leads for sale. 41

Anything you found on Zillow, FSBO, the MLS or similar 3rd party real estate website. 43

Anything sourced from public notices. 44

Online advertising for leads. 44

How To Source These Off-Market Leads And What To Do With The Data. 46

Courts we're interested in 47

Case or Document types we're looking for 48

Property appraiser or Tax assessor website 50

Land records/register of deeds 51

Who's who in civil court documents? Untangling Grantor, Grantee, Plaintiff, Defendant, Deceased, Petitioner, Personal Rep, etc... 52

Priority of Liens 53

General Overview Of The Foreclosure Process And Opportunities 57

Types of Foreclosures by State 58

Judicial Foreclosure 59

Non-Judicial or Statutory Foreclosure 64

Using Quit Claim Deeds To Purchase Off-Market Properties: 66

Assigning Contracts Versus Double Closing 68

Phase II – Nuts and Bolts of Building a Professional Wholesaling Operation from Scratch 71

Setting Up Your Outreach Program And Sales Backend. 71

Don't put off your LLC filing 71

Finding the right closing agent 72

Skip Tracing 73

Find quality virtual assistants 73

Field Rep to take on-site video 74

Website 75

CRM 76
  Communications 77
Workflow: Putting It All Together 78
  Take your snail mail campaigns to the next level 79
  Follow up schedule and content 81
  Stages of the pipeline 83
Filtering And Prioritizing Leads. 85
Finding The Property's Real Wholesale Value 88
  Comparative Market Analysis (CMA): Note - this is different for wholesalers than regular investors. 89
  Example Comp Evaluation: 93
  Current Market Value (CMV): 94
  After Repair Value (ARV): 95
Screening Leads To Determine Your Max And Initial Offer. 96
  Finding your max offer for a quick flip or if you don't know what the end buyer's goals are: 99
Phase III - Locking Down Contracts 102
Initial Outreach To Sellers 102
  Contacting attorneys versus owner/rep directly 102
  Proof of funds request 103
  Primary goals on the first phone call 104
General Rules For Contacting Sellers: 105
Sample Scripts And Mailings 108
  Cold Contact Direct Mail Flyer (Foreclosure) 108
  Cold Contact Direct Mail Flyer (Probate) 109
  For SMS and Voicemail 110
  Message to subject: 110
  Message to other relative if you don't receive a call back: 110
  First contact by voice (pre-foreclosure) 111

First contact by voice (probate) 111
Adapting on the fly to common interruptions 112
Distressed Homeowner Common Objections and Solutions 115
Owner understands how much equity they have in the home and refuses to sell at a steep discount. 115
Owner flat out says they have no interest in moving, no matter what price you offer. 116
Homeowner wants to sell but lacks the financial means to relocate. 118
Owner suggests some sort of alternative financing/purchasing scheme. 119
Owner tries to start a bidding war. 119
A married couple hold joint title. One wants to take your offer, but the other doesn't. 121
Owner has long since moved away and stopped paying the mortgage, while renting the home out. 121
Probate Common Objections and Responses: 122
It's not my property yet, it's my (deceased relative). 122
I don't know if we're going to sell the house... (or general indecisiveness/noncommittal to any course of action). 122
I'd like to sell immediately, but (other family member) wants (something else). 123
I'd like to sell, but I (or another) family member is currently living there and can't afford/doesn't want to move out. 123
What's this lowball offer? I'm not selling for less than... (any attempt to negotiate price). 123
They don't have the slightest interest in a cash offer. Savvy seller that wants to take the property to the broad market. 124
Key Follow Up Questions Before Sending The Contract 124
Post-Contact But Pre-Signing Due Diligence 127
Recognizing Potential Code Violations. 129
How To Get Out Of Those Bidding Wars. 131

  Risk Management - Key Clauses In The Wholesale Contract 133
Phase IV – Finding and Working with End Buyers 136
  Locating And Qualifying Cash Buyers Fast 136
    1) Auction winners. 138
    2) Active flippers. 140
  Introducing Yourself To New Cash Buyers 142
  What To Ask Your Potential End Buyers. 143
  How To Get Fast Engagement For Your Deal. 144
  Your Assignment Offer 146
    Sample Prospectus 149
  Final Thoughts And Encouragement 150
About the Author 152

Don't forget to check out the free hour-long companion video to this book on my website. Since it's so much easier to show, rather than tell, I put together a big picture video overview that covers everything you're reading here, from A-Z, on some real-world examples.

Real estate is all about building relationships, which is why I love nothing more than chatting all day. Please shoot me any questions, concerns or random thoughts you have and I'll respond as fast as possible.

www.lirankoren.com

www.luxurypropertycare.com

Common Misunderstandings About Wholesaling Real Estate

What Precisely Are We Talking About By Wholesaling? How Easy Is It In Practice?

Hands down the greatest misconception that shatters the dreams of so many new wholesalers is the fantasy that this is an "easy source of income and a great way to get started in real estate without any capital."

Never mind all the hype you might have read online; just think about how that statement defies common sense. Wholesaling is not some exotic, special field of real estate that's above all the rules, but rather an unofficial label used to describe an investor who doesn't close on the property themselves.

Sounds great on the surface. I mean, you're not putting up your own money or taking legal ownership of anything, so what could go wrong? But that mindset glosses over some huge stumbling blocks that even bedevil the pros:

A wholesaler still needs to find and lock down ultra-discounted deals that no one else has been able to yet, and then figure out how to sell that contract to a 3rd party.

In other words, you're still doing everything else that a regular investor would do to secure these great investments in the first place, plus the additional step of convincing someone else to buy into your "fabulous" deal. Double the work. So how can this strategy be easier than simply buying the property yourself or investing in a REIT?

A professional wholesaler is not some middleman/woman that's slipping into a real estate transaction in the hopes of skimming off a little profit while putting in the bare-minimum effort. Such wannabe "wholesalers" crash and burn fast. They make grandiose promises to sellers, but then can't find buyers for the overpriced properties they have under contract. Or these amateurs spray and pray thousands of low-ball purchase offers around, only getting responses from the most desperate sellers. Then they wonder why it's so hard to resell a dilapidated property saddled with code violations in a bad neighborhood for a fee high enough to cover their expenses.

These folks that don't have a plan and aren't willing to buckle down and do their due diligence homework rarely succeed in assigning any contracts that close on time. After a month or two, they give up—bitter and angry after throwing away thousands of dollars on wasted marketing efforts.

Not that there aren't plenty of wholesalers without any formal real estate training making a killing in this niche, but they didn't get there easily. The only successful wholesalers I've ever met are working their butts off even harder than me to find distressed sellers that no one else knows about and then matching them up with the right buyers. They earn every penny of their assignment fee. They're going cross-eyed staring at Excel spreadsheets and crunching the numbers all day. These wholesalers are going the extra mile to create win-win-win situations, and they sure don't have any illusions about this being an easy "gig."

I'm not trying to de-motivate you, but you didn't buy this book for a generic rah-rah pep talk. You wanted to know what problems you'll be facing and how to overcome them. So here's the cold hard truth:

Making a living as a wholesaler is *far* more complicated than getting your real estate license and listing properties for sale, or even directly flipping properties with your own capital. Let's recap all the major steps involved so you understand exactly what you're getting into:

1. The only way to find the steeply discounted properties you need to make a profit is by working off-market real estate. If the property is already for sale somewhere, even FSBO, then competitors will drive up the price too high for a wholesaler.

2. And that's only the beginning. You can't just contact any random homeowner that might want to sell their property but hasn't listed it on the MLS yet. If there's no external pressure to sell now, the

owner's price point will be too high for wholesaling. You have to dig up truly distressed, motivated sellers that are willing to surrender a large chunk of the equity they've built up over years of mortgage payments.

3. Then you have to negotiate with the seller to get the price down to well below the property's market value, the exact opposite of what an agent promises in order to land a contract. You also have to get the price lower than a direct investor could offer, if you want to get your "cut" out of the deal.

4. In order to make sure cash buyers will even consider purchasing your contract, you have to perform extensive due diligence on the property and title just like any investor. Which is something that a listing agent isn't responsible for.

5. Once you've secured a deal, you then have to hunt down and vet reliable cash buyers who can close lightning fast, and not just place a listing to find any retail buyer on the MLS like an agent does.

6. After you've found these reliable 3rd party investors, you have to perform a whole new set of marketing to gain their trust and sell the contract to them. And by the way, these quality buyers aren't inexperienced newbies. They're sophisticated investors paying in cash, so they're expecting a great deal, know exactly how to spot one and won't settle for anything less.

7. If you're assigning contracts instead of double closing like most wholesalers, then your maximum earnings per deal are capped. So you have to repeat this process over and over on a consistent basis if you plan on making serious "quit your day job" money.

8. Oh, and you're doing all of this while facing an ungodly amount of competition and tight deadlines.

So does any of this still sound like a get-rich-quick scheme?

But if you're not discouraged so far and you're still reading along while brainstorming how you can solve these challenges, then you're the type of person who will be fun to work with. Because Lord knows, this business isn't for everyone. Wholesaling is a job for pros, or at least those with the hunger and passion to go pro in a hurry.

It takes a special kind of ambitious entrepreneur to go beyond the simple steps of getting their real estate license and listing inventory for sale. If you just want to dip your toes in the water and "get a feel" for real estate investing, then save yourself the stress and go buy property from an existing wholesaler in your market.

Now, that doesn't mean wholesaling can't be incredibly lucrative and relatively low stress at the same time. There are thousands of investors assigning contracts full-time around the country and love what they do. I've trained up dozens of them myself, but their success didn't come overnight. I've even worked with some part-timers that manage to wholesale multiple contracts every month, while still working their day jobs full-time.

But don't be fooled into thinking any of this is easy. In all of those successful cases, it took persistence, dedication and quite a bit of painful entrepreneurship for them to reach that level. Specifically, we had to solve four major problems before their wholesaling business could take off and deliver consistent returns:

1. Find a steady, cost-effective and renewable source of distressed seller leads. A high-quality list with as few dead ends as possible, but still coming in high enough volume that we can contact several hundred sellers monthly and get dozens of new deals in the pipeline every month.

2. Guarantee these leads are ultra-fresh so that you're one of the first investors to contact the seller. Just getting to the front of the line is half the sales battle won right there.

3. Gather enough information on the property and seller's financial situation so that you can place an initial offer with confidence within the first five seconds of the call. This simple technique is a gamechanger that ramps up engagement exponentially and usually preempts future bidding wars.

4. Find, vet and sell yourself to a steady supply of experienced and deep-pocked cash investors that will buy your contracts fast. As in less than 72 hours. The type of top tier investors who are used

to working with rehab-heavy properties, purchasing from wholesalers and won't leave you hanging at closing.

And that's what this book is all about. No more, but definitely no less. To solve these problems in any market so you can hit the ground running and get those first 100 deals in the pipeline within 90 days. If you're willing to put in the work, then I'll make sure you get the maximum return on every dollar and hour you invest in this business.

Then in a few months, you can thank me by assigning a few juicy contracts my way!

If This Business Is So Competitive, What Chance Do I Have?

While wholesaling is more complicated and research-intensive than most people believe, the so-called competition will be the least of your worries in a few hours. Even if you have zero real estate experience right now, if you follow just 10% of the best practices in this book, you'll instantly be operating way above the average wholesaler's skill level on day one.

If you're new to real estate investing or you're worried about the competition, stop reading right now and go online. Google "we buy houses in cash" and choose any of the millions of results. Go ahead, fill out their cash offer form. Give them your address and contact details (preferably a disposable VOIP number and email to cut down on the spam).

Then sit back and take a look at the jaw dropping unprofessionalism of the so-called "outreach" you get in response. The generic messages asking you for information you already provided, the desperate aggressiveness, the endless spelling errors... and God help you if you actually answer the phone and talk to one of these wholesalers!

Despite you contacting them first and filling out a questionnaire, the rep on the phone doesn't know the first darn thing about your property and financial situation. Maybe you can hear them reading Zillow under their breath, but they have no idea what your comps are and haven't searched for liens, unpaid taxes, building permits, etc...

They don't have the slightest clue what your breakeven point is or what their max offer should be. They're shooting from the hip and asking *you* how much you want for the property, rather than giving a well-informed quote that guarantees they'll be able to sell the contract with reasonable profit. How are they supposed to earn a consistent income that way?

After a half hour on the phone with these buyers, if you haven't hung up already in disgust at the cheesy, high pressure sales tactics, all you've accomplished is getting a ridiculous low-ball cash offer for 50% of your home's value. Sure, if you're willing to call back and sit through another hour of hemming and hawing, then they might raise the price to 60%. Maybe even 70%, if you're willing to waste more of your time scheduling walk throughs and meeting face to face with "acquisition managers."

And if you never respond back? Well, that's how these sites make the real money. The wholesaler just resells your name and address as a "lead" to some other even less experienced wholesaler, who then resells your contact info again after you've ignored their first ten typo-ridden text messages. And so on and so on, with increasingly desperate and even less professional salespeople spamming you for years to come.

And yes, these poor fools keep trying forever. I did this same thing three years ago to see if my competitors were doing anything special. I'm a three-year-old lead, yet I'm still getting fresh phone calls and emails every week to my test Gmail account from new wholesalers that think they just bought a "hot lead" from someone else.

Sorry to put you through that experience, but now you can understand how exasperating it is for someone who's really a motivated seller to deal with these people. So when you call the seller up and know everything about their situation and can make a high-quality offer with confidence, it's a relief for them to talk with a real pro. Even a pleasure.

So do you think they're ever going to call those other buyer's back?

I Don't Know If This Is Right For Me. I've Heard A Lot Of Negative Things About Wholesalers.

It might seem at first glance like wholesalers and brokers/agents will always fight like cats and dogs. Afterall, aren't they competitors? Aren't real estate pros always complaining about wholesalers being a bunch of unprofessional cowboys, at best? At worst, modern-day pirates stealing their business by buying and selling properties off-market.

It's true that real estate pros are used to a more sophisticated, "gentlemanly" game of partnering with other brokers and taking their time to shop properties around to drive up the price, all while spreading the commission wealth.

Conversely, wholesalers tend to view agents as a bunch of elitist, busy body middlemen and women who make things unnecessarily complicated and expensive. Since postings on real estate investing communities are dominated by pros trying to build their brand reputation, it's no wonder you hear only half the story.

Truth is, both groups serve a valuable role. Wholesalers add liquidity and bring new inventory to an otherwise reactive and segmented marketplace, while agents provide unique local market insight and create new value out of thin air by driving up prices.

Or to put it more cynically, **licensed agents service sellers** (no matter the type of listing agreement), since their profit comes from how high the final price is, while **wholesalers service buyers**, since their profit increases the more cheaply they can purchase a property. Call it the yen and yang of real estate, but both groups are vital to keeping the market healthy.

For example, my business relies on wholesalers to bring in the inventory and brokers to unlock maximum value once we're done rehabbing. They aren't in competition with one another, but rather in a perfectly symbiotic relationship. Every contract a wholesaler brings me is a new listing for one of my agents later. And every successful sale an agent arranges leaves me with a pile of cash I need to reinvest quickly to take advantage of the 1031 exchanges. So then I start calling up my wholesaler network, desperate for a ready-made deal that just needs an hour of due diligence and my signature. And so on and so on.

I'm not trying to shake your confidence. I hope if you understand the prejudices facing wholesalers, you'll be even more confident. Because as a wholesaler, you will never enjoy the benefit of the doubt like a licensed agent or broker is often afforded. There are just too many amateur or outright fraudulent actors in this industry for anyone to stake you any sort of trust. Your credibility and reputation extend only as far as your last deal. And no matter how forthright you are, some real estate professionals will always look down on you as an unnecessary middleman (while never seeing the irony in their disdain, but I digress).

But shake it off and never let them see you sweat. Because, again, wholesalers are an integral part of the real estate industry. Wholesalers close hundreds of thousands of deals every year that otherwise wouldn't have happened and unlock billions in equity that would otherwise be wiped out in court or auction proceedings. Since no broker or agent is motivated to get the lowest possible price on a property for their client, wholesalers generate much needed competition and liquidity in the marketplace that no one else can provide. To say nothing about serving as angel investors to distressed home sellers and saving countless families from credit and life destroying foreclosures, or money pit properties draining all their cash with no end in sight.

Enough theory and justifications. At the end of the day, the only person you have to impress is the final buyer. The cash investor signing your assignment agreement only cares about which middleman or woman brings them the best deal. Office politics and market theory don't concern them. They just want to make some money. So if you make that happen, you'll have their respect and their business for years to come.

How Much Can I Realistically Earn By Wholesaling?

The traditional figure you've probably seen quoted is between $5k - $10k per assignment deal. And while that range is quite typical, it's far from the average. I've seen wholesalers earn as little as $1k and as much as $40k on each assignment. There's infinite variance in compensation, since it all depends upon the market value of the property, how much equity is in the deal and, of course, your own sales skills. And if you're doing double closings, you're really flipping a property, so the sky's the limit there.

But how much you make per deal is a poor measure of success. About as useful as asking McDonald's how much they earn from each French Fry they sell. All that matters are how many deals you can pour into your pipeline. We'll cover the specifics of how to keep the pipeline flowing and scale up your business with minimum stress later.

Is Wholesaling Legal In My State? I Don't Have A Real Estate License.

If you've tried to Google this simple question, you've probably seen 10 different real estate pros give 11 different opinions. It's maddening how much conflicting information there is about this straightforward question. But rest assured, it's not a question of whether or not your particular state forbids or condones real estate wholesaling.

The confusion here comes from terminology and not local laws. "Wholesaling" is not a generally recognized real estate legal term, so naturally there's no state, local or Federal statue stating whether or not this practice is legal. Some states have tight regulations regarding how buyers can approach sellers and how contracts can be worded, for example, but there's no way to ban or condone the nebulous concept of wholesaling when there's no way to legally define it.

"Wholesaling" is simply an informal and often emotionally charged label used to describe the larger business model behind the routine transactions of assigning a contract or simultaneous (double) closing. So that's why no lawyer can give you a simple "yes" or "no" answer as to whether this practice is legal. Every attorney you ask will say, "Well, it all depends upon *how* you do it..."

For example, there's no law saying you can't drive from one place to another, regardless of your intent. The cops couldn't care less where you were heading or why, but you can bet they'll pull you over for an expensive chat if they see you going 90 through a school zone.

So while there might be local speed limits governing what wording you can use in your marketing or some other road sign to obey, **assigning a real estate purchase contract to a 3rd party end buyer is 100% legal in every state**.

It's also a routine business practice. You're not doing anything out of the ordinary nor legally dubious. You're not operating in some grey area of the law. All you're doing is making a formal offer to purchase a property to a seller, using a standard residential "as is" sales contract. This already includes time limited contingency clauses that you must close or assign the contract to another buyer within X days. To avoid confusion, you'll make it clear to the seller that one of your "partners" will be closing on the deal and not yourself, but there's nothing exotic about the process, paperwork or end result.

Now, where some wholesalers get into trouble is not because they assigned a contract that they didn't have the money to buy or never even intended to purchase, but because they engaged in some other prohibited activities during that otherwise perfectly legal process. These legal landmines can be divided into three broad categories:

1. Practicing real estate brokering without a license.

2. Using deceptive, misleading or otherwise prohibited marketing to sellers or buyers.

3. Failing to comply with some detail of state, county or municipal law governing local real estate transactions.

Obviously, you need to make sure you're working with a real estate attorney who has experience closing on wholesale deals in your area. While only a good local attorney can cover all the legal minutia, here are the most frequent reasons new wholesalers run afoul of the law.

You'll find that the common theme in each scenario is just a lack of transparency. After all, in every aspect of real estate law, failing to disclose something you should have reasonably known is treated the same as intentional deceit.

Examples of brokering real estate without a license:

- Misrepresenting yourself, either intentionally or through omission, as an "agent," "representative" or similar party acting on behalf of the buyer or seller. You are an independent investor who represents just yourself. To avoid this, I recommend simply mentioning that the end buyer is one of your "partner investors."

- Accepting a commission instead of a flat rate assignment fee from the end buyer. Any percentage cut of the transaction, no matter how you word it, is a commission, which are reserved for licensed agents.

- Not securing a binding purchase contract first from the seller and instead accepting a finder's fee or similar payment "under the table" from the buyer for bringing them a lead. In short, you can sign a purchase agreement with the seller and then assign the contract to a buyer, or give away all the lead's information for free, but nothing in between or else you're acting as an unlicensed broker.

    The only exceptions would be rental agreement listings, property management or related housing/credit service referrals that don't involve brokering a sale. Even then, there are often limits to how much you can earn in referral fees in each state.

Examples of deceptive/prohibited marketing:

- Marketing the property to buyers as if you owned it already, rather than making it 100%, unambiguously clear that you only have the property under contract to purchase and want to assign that contract to a 3rd party. In my experience, this is the most common mistake new wholesalers make.

    It's a silly, high-risk thing to do, since buyers don't care that you're a wholesaler as long as there's equity in the deal. End buyer investors just want to gather inventory cheaply and legally. They don't care about anything else. All the chicanery and subterfuge only complicates things and makes it hard to trust a wholesaler, no matter how great the deal is.

- Deceiving the seller or buyer into believing that there are no other parties involved in the transaction, whether intentionally or through omission.

- Marketing yourself or your company as a way to "prevent foreclosure" or providing some other financing/credit/ housing help. In most states, these industries are tightly regulated. Which means there's strict verbiage required to make it clear that the homeowner is selling the property and will not continue to own it after the transaction is complete.

- Any sort of "bait and switch" advertising, no matter how subtle. The seller should know right off the bat that you want to buy their property. In addition, potential buyers should know immediately what you're offering and what your role is in the transaction.

Examples of failing to comply with state, county or municipal real estate transaction laws:

- Failing to provide all required disclosures when signing the contract or using incorrect verbiage in the purchase agreement. This is the second most common mistake new wholesalers make. **Never download some general form from the internet. Save yourself the headache and legal liability by getting a local real estate attorney to handle your paperwork.**

- Ignoring local notification requirements, such as the Tenant's Right of First Refusal, if required in a particular city.

- In some rare jurisdictions, failing to provide an adequate earnest money deposit or accepting too large of an assignment fee.

Yeah, I know. A lot of little details, but the key thing is that in each of these scenarios **the act of assigning the purchase contract, regardless of why the wholesaler did so, is 100% legal**.

All of these problems can be avoided by simply being fully transparent with the seller and buyer, and talking with a local real estate attorney to make sure you've crossed all your t's and dotted all the i's. Just like with any business. That's all you have to do to stay on the right side of the law and spend your time on the important things that make you money.

I Don't Know. I Feel Uncomfortable Hunting Down People Going Through Hard Times So I Can Buy Their House Cheaply. That Just Feels Wrong.

When I say wholesalers and direct cash buyers are angel investors, I'm not being cute. Nor trying to rationalize things. We're honestly providing a hard to find and desperately needed service, even if we're doing it solely for profit and not out of the kindness of our hearts.

Now, I'm not going to give you some abstract moral lesson here, but rather prove my point with a simple fact:

I've closed on well over 1,000 properties going through foreclosure, pre-foreclosure, divorce or probate in the last ten years. I've lost track of how many tens of thousands of cold calls I've made or listened to my sales team make to seal those deals. Yet in all those contacts with sellers, I've heard them say "No thanks," or ask for more money or different contract terms, but I've never once heard a single lead get angry or offended that we contacted them out of the blue while they were in a bad financial place.

When we finally meet in person down at the title attorney's office for closing, I've never been met with a scowl or a cold stare. I'm always greeted with a hearty handshake and, more often than not, a tear-filled hug. So what if we made some money in the process? All that matters to the homeowner is that we fixed the greatest financial disaster they've ever faced.

I didn't come up with the term "angel investor." It wasn't until I heard, "you're an angel" or "God must have sent you," a hundred times that it really sank in how I was providing a lot more than just money. I was saving the day. Giving these people and their families a second chance before the soulless bank came and took everything they had worked so hard to build.

And soon you'll be called a hero as well.

To be clear: even my ego isn't big enough to think that I'm "a gift from God." My motivation is simply to make some money… but thank God we live in a country where you can get rich and help people at the same time. Real estate is one of those rare industries where unbridled capitalism does more good than harm… but I'm getting off track. There's some prep work we need to square away before we can enjoy the fruits of our labors.

Phase I – Laying The Foundation for Lasting Success

This preparation section is crucial to your lasting success, so please don't skip over it to get to the action steps. Understanding the ins and outs of how you source your leads will save you a fortune in the long run, as well as spare you countless hours chasing down, qualifying and staging dead end leads.

The Keys To Wholesaling Like A Boss

Let's face it, everyone and their cousin is playing the wholesaling game nowadays. And most of these wholesalers think they're offering sellers something special with their promises of "paying in cash," or "purchasing in as-is condition, and with fast closing."

But so what? Yawn. Taking the property in its current state, closing within five business days and delivering a certified cashier's check into escrow on the same day as signing the contract are table stakes in this business. Where's your edge? What makes you stand out from everyone else spouting the same lines?

How to find distressed sellers before anyone else.

The only way to consistently produce an endless number of quality leads is to scan pending court records (not public records) for the most motivated sellers. These are people with the greatest and most pressing problems that we can solve today. Now, that might not sound special, since everyone is looking for the same type of lead, but we're sourcing these leads at a different time than everyone else. We're getting to them before any public notice is filed and long before they show up in any lead subscription service. Even just a few days head start over every other investor changes the game for you. I'll go over the types of leads we're looking for and exactly how to find them in the next chapter.

Fair warning though: this research is a lot of boring, eye-straining work. Even in a middle-sized metropolitan area with a healthy local economy, you'll still have hundreds of Tier 1 foreclosure and probate cases to sift through every month. Not counting thousands of Tier 2 leads, like evictions and pre-foreclosure flags. But whether you automate the process with web scrapers, hire an assistant or do everything yourself, it's absolutely necessary to do this homework if you want to have any edge over the competition.

No more driving for dollars or sending mailings to every door in a zip code hoping to scrounge up the 1% of motivated sellers in a neighborhood. Instead, you can weed out 99% of homeowners in an area and target that 1% of ultra-motivated sellers with laser accuracy and never-ending precision. Besides saving you a fortune on marketing costs, the extra information you'll extract from the courthouse and tax rolls will drastically increase your conversion rate.

Best of all, since these leads are so fresh that the seller hasn't even been formally served yet, you can skip to the head of the line and usually be the first investor to contact these folks. That's half the sales battle won right there.

How to gain that all-important negotiating leverage with sellers.

At the end of the day, this whole business comes down to convincing a total stranger to sell you their property for much less than the market value. If you master that skill, then everything else are just details.

And no, there is no full proof "system" to winning on every sales call. Even if you are the first investor to call them. In fact, if the seller is too eager and wants to sign immediately without serious dickering over price or terms, then you should pump the brakes and double check all your numbers. You must be missing something. Odds are there's something really wrong with the property or you're offering too much money.

In a normal sale, it generally takes a bare minimum of three phone calls to get them to sign on the dotted line. The initial outreach, which usually ends with us sending them "more information." Best case scenario that's a sample purchase agreement to read over. At least one more follow up call later in the next day or two to haggle over price and answer procedural questions. Then a final reassurance call when they're ready to sign and to set a closing date. And that's not even counting back and forth emails or additional calls if they get cold feet.

But don't worry about that yet, because it's the initial phone call that matters the most. If you can get them in the pipeline, odds are they're going to stay there. Or to put it another way, it's much easier to smooth over seller remorse or amend contract terms to keep a seller happy than it is to get them signed in the first place.

With that said, there are quite a few things we can do to stack the deck in your favor during that first phone call. Simple steps that will make you stand out from any other wannabe buyer and give you the advantage when it comes time to butt heads over price.

Because it's all about who holds the data advantage. For example, these court records we're going over will show you how much the seller is in debt for. So you'll know their bottom-line price. When combined with a wholesaler-unique CMA and ARV that we'll do later, you can estimate an initial and max offer amount to within +/- 5%. All before you've seen the property or even picked up the phone.

This might sound like a lot of work in preparation for a cold call, but it saves you time in the long run. Yes, you'll spend a few more minutes researching each lead to figure out your initial offer before reaching out, but you'll save countless hours of phone time.

For example, the typical wholesaler will average 30 minutes on the phone with each contact just to qualify the owner as interested in selling near the wholesaler's price range, learning more about their situation to get a feel for their minimum price, and then staging the prospect for the hard sale. That's not counting time for negotiating or asking due diligence questions, but just getting ready to make an offer in the first place. When the wholesaler gets around to naming a price, most of the sellers get frustrated and abandon the call because they were expecting a higher figure. Especially after investing so much time telling a total stranger their life story. So if that wholesaler had 10 leads to contact today and only half were willing to sell within an acceptable price range, this wholesaler just spent five hours preparing five deals for the hard sales pitch.

However, you'll invest ten minutes researching each lead ahead of time so you can qualify and stage them within seconds. If they're still on the phone after you give your initial purchase offer, then by definition they are interested in selling near your price point. Now you can jump straight into the negotiating phase. And if they hang up right after you quote your price, well, they would have done so eventually. Best to get them out of the way now and focus on the next lead. You just saved a bunch of time that would have been spent chasing down a dead end. So if you had 10 leads to contact and only half were willing to sell in your price range, you've prepped all five for the final sales pitch with less than two hours of research and call time.

Or to put the time savings another way, you can work 2.5 times as many leads a day using this approach than with traditional wholesaler strategies.

And the same goes for your mailing campaigns when you can include an initial offer amount. The only homeowners calling you back will be those still interested after receiving your below-market rate offer. They'll naturally try to get you to raise your price, but you know right off the bat that your offer is at least close to what they consider acceptable. You're in the right ballpark and can now spend your time negotiating brass tacks.

As game changing as all that is, increased efficiency is only the beginning. When you've taken a few minutes to look up court records, liens and find comps and work up your own CMA, then you hold the information advantage in the negotiation phase. You can adjust your offer with confidence by just gathering a little more due diligence information. There's absolutely no reason you can't secure all your deals exclusively over the phone and send your field team out later to record videos for end buyers. Which will give you an even bigger advantage over all those other wholesalers that tell sellers, "I need to run the numbers and get back to you" or schedule a time to come by in person before signing the deal.

Sellers will respond to your confidence and how easy it is to work with you. Maybe they could squeeze a few more percentage points out of someone else, but time is short and their patience is wearing thin. That's when you'll have a true edge over any of your "competitors." Those others can call themselves investors, but you're the only real estate pro on the phone. The only one that knows all about the seller's situation and already made them a reasonable offer that could make all their problems go away today. After hearing from you, they won't have any interest in following up with those other buyers who can only send an insulting, low ball offer on first contact.

And if your potential seller isn't so impatient and wants to shop your offer around? Even better. Other wholesalers will assume the offer isn't legitimate, just a negotiating tactic, and will insist on a face-to-face meeting and walk-through of the property before they can even consider topping that price.

Just more work. More stress. More delays. Remember, we're not bothering with properties that are already listed for sale. We're working the distressed seller circuit where time is running out for the homeowner. No matter what other quotes they're hearing, you're still the only investor around that's willing to make all the seller's problems go away today, without any more hassle.

How to vet your buyers as thoroughly as your sellers so you're only working with the most reliable partners.

One of the biggest things holding back wholesalers from scaling their business is they tend to cast a wide net and send their wholesale deals out to anyone that will listen. They're confusing wholesale with retail sales. So they spend precious time hunting for customers, rather than *clients*. This seemingly small distinction is crucial if you want to assign contracts on a regular basis and have them close as fast as possible.

A **customer** needs to be converted, which takes extra time and energy. You have to persuade the customer to purchase any sort of real estate right now, then make them want to purchase this type of product, and finally convince them to buy from you. And even after you've jumped through all those hoops, there's no way to tell if they have the means and will to close on the deal. If financing will fall through or they'll otherwise get cold feet. You might recognize all of this as what a real estate agent does to earn their commission, but as a wholesaler, you should be targeting a different type of clientele.

A **client**, on the other hand, is an established business that's looking for a vender to supply them with quality inventory on a regular basis. Whether a single investor or large organization, these potential clients are already buying distressed real estate in the area. All you have to show them is that they should buy from you, because you're a reliable partner that can supply steady inventory for their business at a provable discount.

It's important to focus on finding clients over customers not just for the repeat business, but also because the clock's ticking. As soon as you sign that purchase agreement with a seller, it's too late to start looking for buyers. You need to have a short list of pre-vetted buyers on hand before you ever pick up the phone and start calling sellers.

We'll cover the details about locating, vetting and contacting these top-tier end buyers in the last chapter of this book. In broad strokes though, you'll source your cash buyer list from active and successful auction bidders, as well as active flippers already working with distressed properties in the neighborhood.

This ensures your buyers:

1) Are actively looking for property in the area right now.

2) Have sufficient cash or hard money/private credit available to close fast.

3) Have experience with distressed, off-market properties, so they won't be skittish about repairs and rehab.

When you're only dealing with these types of experienced investors instead of any random retail buyer, you can assign each contract within 72 hours of getting the seller's signature on it. Quite often, even on the same day, once you've established your credentials and proven your worth. Then you can spend the vast majority of your time contacting sellers and feeding properties into your pipeline, rather than waste time coddling amateur end buyers all the way through closing.

Adopting a high-volume mindset to take your game to the next level.

The most successful wholesalers, just like the most successful agents, know that it's not about how much you make per deal, but how many deals you can sign. The most famous brokers out there never have to show a house themselves. They're locking down listing agreements daily and assigning or referring the grunt work to the less famous agents.

If you're wholesaling by assigning contracts, then you most definitely need to adopt this mindset. There's only so much you can earn on a deal, and it's usually less than the commission a broker receives. So in order to turn a large and regular profit, you need to close as many deals as possible, as fast as you can. Once you fully accept this concept though, you'll have a massive advantage over every other wholesaler out there.

Because in practice, this means you're willing to make your max purchase offer higher than the average wholesaler because you can accept a lower assignment fee from buyers. It might seem counter-intuitive to leave money on the table, but this is real estate. The more you share the wealth, the more wealth you have access to. For example, if you never purchase a property for more than 60% of the ARV and never accept less than $10k in assignment fees, then you're making far more on each deal as a wholesaler that's willing to pay homeowners 70% of their ARV and assign the contract for just $5k.

But the second "discount" wholesaler is going to net 10x as much income for the year, while dealing with a fraction of the stress. The first penny-pinching wholesaler is hustling every day to close on a handful of deals a year, spending countless hours in hardball negotiations with sellers and buyers. However, the one willing to share the wealth is signing purchase contracts with ease and in high volume. And the cash buyers don't cringe when the wholesaler calls, but instead pro-actively call them up and ask, "Hey, you got any more of those quick flips handy? I need to make some fast cash. Come on, don't hold out on me. I know you've always got inventory to move."

What Makes A Legitimate Wholesale Lead?

With the wholesaler's unique business model, simply finding a homeowner that's tempted to sell but hasn't yet listed their property on the market isn't enough to qualify them as a lead. You're not a buyer's agent who will profit at any price point. Without a steep discount from the seller, you'll never find a reliable end buyer, and never see your payday. So you need a way to make sure you're only talking to people that are under serious pressure to sell quickly and at rates well below market value.

Many new wholesalers don't appreciate how absolutely vital it is to approach the right leads at the *right time*. Timing is the be all and end all factor in this business. Maybe it's not quite a, "If you're not first, you're last," situation, but darn close. In my experience, if you're not one of the first three buyers to contact a lead, then you're wasting your time calling them.

I don't care if you have a silver tongue; someone else is always smoother. Your sales skills don't mean anything unless you're one of the first investors to contact a lead. Otherwise, the seller is going to be too experienced with all the wholesaler scripts. They'll be too jaded and impatient to give you a chance to lay on the charm, and just cut you off to find out your max price.

So if you want to get the maximum return on your marketing budget and avoid the bidding wars, every lead you work needs to meet the following bare-minimum criteria, or else it's not worth your time:

1. The seller must be facing some form of financial distress that makes them open to selling for less than market value. Duh, obviously you don't want to buy at market prices, but that's just the beginning...

2. The property cannot yet be listed for sale anywhere. This is so often overlooked. It doesn't matter how you sourced the property or how distressed the seller is if it's already up for sale. If it's on Zillow, the MLS or FSBO, the competition will bid up the price to near market levels. In short, when you check a potential seller's property online, every site should say "not for sale." Then you know you're onto something. Now you just need to make sure you get to them early…

3. You must have a better than even chance to be the first investor to contact this lead. Getting to the front of the line is the difference between closing 10 deals and none this month. In other words, the court record you're sourcing the lead from must be fresh and without any public notice filed yet. We'll get to all of that in the next section.

4. Finally, you must have enough information on the owner and property to estimate your max purchase offer with reasonable confidence *before* contacting the prospect. Being able to offer an actual dollar amount in the opening sentence of your first contact is a gamechanger. This means not only estimating the property's value, but also having a rough estimate of the owner's debt load to find their breakeven price. Then you'll never waste your time sending low-ball offers, while also making sure you don't overbid.

We'll cover deal evaluation and initial offer strategies in more detail during Phase III, but please take a few more minutes to finish the prep work here. Make sure you grasp all the nuance involved with each type of lead so you can understand their pressure points and how you can help.

If any one of the above conditions are not met, then you don't have a high-quality lead. If all four items are checked, then you have a red-hot lead that's worth investing time and money to research their situation, skip trace their contact info and call them up before anyone else does.

We can also refine this basic criterion even further, so you can get into the mindset of your prospects and target your marketing like a sniper:

Classes Of Leads For Wholesalers

Note: The tier status of these leads is based upon a wholesaler's point of view, which is naturally quite relative. Other real estate operators will have different priorities. For example, a licensed sales agent might consider evictions to be a Tier 1 lead, since that's an easy way to land a renter listing agreement, and foreclosures a Tier 2 lead, since they'll be harder to sell for a good commission on the open market. However, a wholesaler will jump at distressed sellers in foreclosure, while considering evictions a lower priority lead only worth pursing if nothing better is available.

Tier 1 – Hot leads

These are homeowners or estate reps that not only fit all of the criteria from above, but are either under a severe time crunch to sell or can't sell without court approval.

Early Foreclosures

The key to working this niche is timing. A lead here isn't just anyone going through foreclosure, but specifically homeowners in the pre-judgment or pre-notice of sale phase. Meaning the ink is still wet on the Lis Pendens or trustee sale notice. It'll be weeks to months before these properties show up as a "pre-foreclosure" sale on Zillow or similar sites (Note: Calling this early foreclosure period pre-foreclosure is a misnomer. We'll cover true pre-foreclosures in the Tier 2 lead section).

These people are going to have a hard time fetching fair market value on the MLS, simply because they don't have the luxury of waiting for the best offer to come along. In most cases, they'll also have to invest significant out-of-pocket cash to fix the place up or give huge credits against the selling price. When they do receive a decent offer on the open market, the buyer's lender tends to drag out the underwriting process and requests multiple appraisals or even additional inspections. And every additional day they delay just stacks up more attorney fees and back interest that'll come out of the seller's pocket at closing.

The cold hard reality is if these poor people had the will and wherewithal to sell the property already, or the up-front cash to pay the points on a loan modification, they would have done so before things reached this point. In practice, the only real option for a seller in foreclosure is to find an off-market investor who has the cash or a private line of credit already and can close immediately. An angel investor who can save the day, today.

That's your cue.

You'll most often find these opportunities in judicial foreclosure states. In those areas, we want to target potential sellers as soon as the initial Lis Pendens (notification of a lawsuit) is recorded, but before the court has awarded a judgment or authorized the plaintiff to schedule an auction. In this early phase, the pressure on the homeowner is really intense, but the competition is still light because no public notice has been issued yet. So it's your time to shine.

In non-judicial (statutory) foreclosure states, it might be difficult to find these before anyone else. More often than not, there's no court involvement in the foreclosure at all, or only when it's time to schedule the auction. By then, the competition will be fierce.

However, sometimes there is a short window when the trustee has to file a Notice of Default with the court or request some other court filing before issuing the public Notice of Sale. So if non-judicial foreclosures are common in your area, talk to a local foreclosure attorney and ask about every document that needs to be recorded at court in this process and the deadlines for each. If you can get to the homeowner just a couple of days before a public notice is made, then you'll have a huge advantage.

Pros:

1) Easy to estimate how much the owner owes and therefore their minimum "break even" sales price before you ever call them. That gives you an immediate edge in negotiations. You'll find all this information in the complaint attached to the case.

If the forecloser is the first lien holder (original mortgage, for example), then they have to sue everyone else to clear out their interest. This means they've already done a preliminary title search and included the results in the complaint. You'll still have to perform your own due diligence before signing the contract, but when doing your initial lead screening, it saves you a ton of time to have all the liens and other parties with interest in the property on a single page.

Note: With all of these liens, make sure they're actually recorded as a lien against the property, rather than a wage garnishment or some other judgment. To safeguard their interests, some lenders will pull a credit report on the homeowner when they begin foreclosure and just name every other creditor they can find as a defendant. So not every entity listed in the complaint will have a lien interest in the property.

2) By the time the foreclosure begins, most of these sellers have already mentally conceded defeat and are psychologically ready to sell. Even if they haven't abandoned the property all together and are still fighting, they're beginning to accept the bleakness of the situation. They've had at least four months in pre-foreclosure to come up with the cash to pay the points on a loan modification plan or fix the place up to sell on the open market. For one reason or another, they could not or would not take these steps.

So now, barring some exceptional circumstances, the best they can hope for is to delay the inevitable. Even the most reluctant sellers are going to be tempted to abandon ship when they see the bank is accelerating their loan and racking up all sorts of inflated fees and back interest to gobble up as much of their equity as possible.

3) Taking advantage of lien priority. I won't go into detail about how to leverage the priority of liens to wipe out the interest of other lien holders and create equity out of thin air. While that's my favorite niche, it doesn't really apply to wholesaling.

However, a wholesaler can still profit from junior lien holders being the first to foreclose on a property. Because the second the senior lien holder (ex. original lender) files a Lis Pendens, the payoff balance is going to balloon with all the court and attorney fees. In many states, the lender might even be entitled to a deficiency judgment to recover all these costs against the seller if the property doesn't fetch enough at auction.

So if you move fast and close the contract before the original lender forecloses, the only extra mortgage costs will be back interest and late fees. Plus no judgment liability later. Pointing this out to the seller gives them a major incentive to sign with you today.

Cons:

1) Need careful due diligence. Obviously, you can expect more rehab work on these ultra-distressed and often vacant properties, but that's only the tip of the iceberg. With the owner's financial situation collapsing, you need to keep checking the local court records for new pending judgments against the property owner all the way up until closing.

There might be active court cases that weren't yet recorded as liens when you signed the contract, but could put the seller underwater on the deal right before closing. You can even have multiple foreclosures going on simultaneously, so you need some deep dive research to make sure you're covering all of the seller's debt. Or else they'll back out at the last minute.

2) Expect to cover all of the cash-strapped seller's closing costs. These are generally higher than average too. The cash needed on closing for the buyer will usually be higher than a traditional sale, since foreclosed properties tend to have large tax defaults that aren't going to be pro-rated.

We'll only be working with end buyers that have bought distressed properties in the past, so this won't be a deal breaker, provided you disclose all hidden costs right off the bat and don't bury them in the fine print. The price you quote your buyer in your prospectus should be all-inclusive.

New Probate Cases

These are simply people, usually but not always heirs, that are petitioning the court for the right to disburse the assets in a deceased person's estate. Regardless of the details, this is an absolute gold mine for wholesalers. At least if you're patient enough to wait for court approval and willing to go the extra mile to help the petitioner fend off creditors and close probate as quickly as possible.

Pros:

1) The estate rep/petitioner for personal representative (PR) status cannot sell the property on the regular market until probate is complete or they receive court approval. So for a little while, you have a captive audience. By the way, the same goes for real estate agents looking to secure future listings with hardly any competition.

2) You can still sign a purchase contract with the rep though, just one with a "contingent on court approval" clause. This approval is going to take several weeks to several months to receive. So unlike every other niche, you'll have ample time to find a buyer that will fetch the highest assignment fee. Or arrange transactional funding for a double close or even finance the purchase as your own investment.

3) These properties generally have much lower debt loads and have been vacant for a while. With all the cash needed to maintain the property in the meantime, extra rehab to get it up to selling standards and the probate legal expenses piled on top, the rep is looking at more immediate financial pressure than most people in foreclosure. It's a perfect recipe for an easy and lucrative wholesale deal.

4) The rep is far less likely to be occupying the property and thus resistant to moving, or having a tenant lease that the buyer will have to honor.

5) While the seller might not be facing a credit-destroying foreclosure, they have an equally challenging financial problem: Coming up with large sums of cash out of pocket to maintain the property and keep the legal process going.

Probate is far from cheap. In most jurisdictions, the basic filing and attorney fees for even simple summary administration will run into several thousands of dollars. The costs can then climb exponentially depending on a million little factors.

And these aren't bills that are due on some future date, but rather hard cash the petitioner needs to pay up front or else the case doesn't proceed. Which leads to so many of these reps falling into the "sunk cost trap." The PR has to keep pumping more cash into the legal slot machine, or else they'll never get permission to sell the property and recoup their previous investments.

Sure, some probate attorneys only require a partial payment up front and will take the bulk of their fee upon the sale of the assets... but in those situations they're drastically inflating their costs and fleecing these poor people even more.

Oh, and we haven't even mentioned the costs of keeping up with any mortgage payments, HOA dues, taxes, insurance, landscaping, maintenance, etc. on the property. So much cash flying out of their pocket every month in the hope that it'll all be worth it someday. So imagine their relief when you call them up and can make an immediate cash offer to take this headache off their hands.

6) With this niche, you'll come across all sorts of unique opportunities that go beyond just residential properties. Some estates have assets that you would never find on the open market, such as owning controlling interest in commercial or industrial properties or land in prime locations. These special deals are usually reserved for well-connected agents to sell... but now you're the one the estate rep trusts and has made a connection with.

Cons:

1) This niche can get complicated in a hurry. There are several types of probate administration, each with their own rules, procedures and time frames. And then each case will progress at different speeds, depending on your state laws, whether the deceased died with or without a will and whether or not heirs are fighting for ownership. As always, I urge you to have an in-depth chat with a local probate attorney, someone likely different than your title attorney, to understand all the ins and outs. The more you know about the process, the more information you can give to sellers and help spark a real conversation.

2) Since there is a sizeable delay between signing and executing the contract, you'll have to monitor the title history on the property on a regular basis. It's quite common for sudden new liens or even foreclosures to be filed against the property while you're under contract, especially since sending out multiple public notices to creditors is a requirement to complete the probate process. By the way, those notices to creditors that are posted in the local newspaper are where most companies selling probate "leads" source their info. Way

too late when a public notice is issued and a wholesaler like yourself has already locked down the contract.

Granted, the seller's debt load is not directly your problem, but you can bet these issues will become your problem fast if you don't stay ahead of them. Even if the petitioner wants to continue with the deal, the court will invalidate the contract if your purchase agreement doesn't cover all the liens. So it's your responsibility to stay abreast of these headwinds, help the petitioner negotiate with creditors and even be ready to renegotiate your own offer.

3) You often have to smooth talk multiple stakeholders in the estate. In other words, sell the deal more than once. You can have more than one person petitioning for joint administrative rights or even rival petitions. Even if there's only one rep, that could be because the other heirs will be signing a QCD transfer of their interest in the property to the family rep in order to sell the property as fast as possible. So while legally the estate rep will have the authority to sell the asset, in practice if any other family member disagrees with the deal then they have several options to throw a wrench into things.

For one small example, I've been in many situations where I've had a great deal signed with the PR that everyone in the family was happy with... only to see some other heir get cold feet at the last minute. Now they're threatening to file a rival admin petition or some other legal maneuver to delay the sale and pressure me into offering more money.

It's usually a bluff, of course, since all this paperwork costs a small fortune. So most of the time the heirs can work this disagreement out amongst themselves. If it's a really good deal with a bunch of equity involved, sure, then I'm willing to budge on pricing.

Otherwise, I'm not going to get involved with inter-family squabbling. I have more important leads to work on. If someone doesn't want to sell, I'm not going to cause problems by trying to enforce the purchase agreement. I'll just shrug and move on to another prospect. Like with any negotiation, if you're not willing to fold and walk away from the table at any time, then you've already lost the game.

Tier 2 – Warm leads

Pre-foreclosures

These are folks that are still in the roughly four-month period between going into default and the lender filing for foreclosure. The term pre-foreclosure might seem quite simple, but everyone has a different definition. Most data brokers call any point before the property is sold at auction "pre-foreclosure," because you can theoretically swoop in at the last second and buy the property off-market. In practice though, anything that's listed as "in pre-foreclosure" on Zillow or some other real estate website is too old for our purposes. There's a good reason it hasn't sold yet, so don't be a sucker.

When I say pre-foreclosure, I mean that the very first step of the foreclosure process has not yet begun. The lender may have issued a default notice to the homeowner, but they have not yet activated their trustee powers (in a non-judicial foreclosure) or filed a Lis Pendens (in a judicial foreclosure). **There is no court record, land record, public notice or anything identifying a property that's truly in pre-foreclosure.** So unless your source works for the bank or knows the homeowner personally, anyone guaranteeing to find pre-foreclosure leads either doesn't understand the process, or they're lying through their teeth.

But all is not lost. While there is no court document that identifies these types of leads with perfect certainty, you can still flag likely pre-foreclosures by how many involuntary liens and certain civil judgments they match. We'll go over them in the next section.

As exciting as this niche appears on the surface, there are two reasons why these aren't guaranteed Tier 1 leads and still need some more research before you can dive in:

- Pre-foreclosures are the hardest to find, especially in non-judicial (statutory) foreclosure states. There usually aren't any direct court records flagging the potential foreclosure, so you have to look at secondary indicators. Such as new HOA/COA liens or property tax defaults. If you see these other signs that the property owner is in distress, then check to see if there are any ongoing foreclosures (we'll cover searching for records in the next chapter, How to Source These Leads).

- Even when you identify the pre-foreclosure properties, there's no guarantee the owner is ready to sell. If they're underwater, the homeowner might be clinging to the hope they can scrounge up the cash for a loan modification or find a short seller.

If there is serious equity involved, like a wholesaler wants to see, then the bank usually pushes hard to start the foreclosure process so they can lock in their inflated judgment costs. Plus, in that situation, with the additional equity at stake and more time to react, the homeowner is more inclined to get a lawyer and fight the bank.

Relevant Types of Liens & Civil Judgments

Technically, you could work each of these liens and judgments as their own niche, but that's incredibly time consuming. When you're first starting out and resources are limited, the most efficient use of your time is to flag pre-foreclosures by any property that shows up in two or more of the following types of lien/judgment searches. And if you're in a non-judicial foreclosure state, this might be the only way to flag pre-foreclosures before the auction is scheduled.

Now, there's a vast collection of liens the government or private parties can put against a property, but most are quite routine. The average lien filed at the courthouse or land records office doesn't tell you anything about the owner's level of financial stress or likelihood that they're ready to sell. However, there are a few types of liens/pending judgments that could signal that a homeowner is in the pre-foreclosure process or is otherwise a motivated seller:

- Miscellaneous civil judgments for large amounts. Primarily business loan defaults, mechanics liens for large amounts, hospital liens or exceptionally high credit card defaults.

  You want to make sure you're not looking at "routine" liens though, such as those from new construction, HELOC or a second mortgage. Just those that are involuntary and involve fairly large sums of money.

- HOA/COA liens of any amount. If they aren't paying the HOA, that's a big red flag they've abandoned the property and/or they're in default on their mortgage.

- Local code violations, especially easy-to-clear issues like nuisance fines. These fines can be particularly onerous, since it can take weeks to months to fix and inspect the violation, all while the fees are accruing daily. So the owner must be facing some serious hardship if they're not clearing these violations fast. Remember though, we're only looking for fresh fines and not old ones.

Many fix and flip investors work long-term code violations as its own niche, but that area is more difficult for wholesalers to profit from. There's usually a reason the property hasn't yet been gobbled up by another investor after all this time. You'll find yourself chasing down many dead ends in this niche. Often the owner is extremely difficult to find or there are some hard-to-clear title issues.

- County/State/Federal unpaid taxes. Ideally you want to target these while they're still listed as in default but not yet recorded as a lien. Alone, a tax lien doesn't tell you much, because they often aren't recorded until months or a year after default, but if it's combined with another involuntary lien, then the chance the home is in default or close to it is quite high.

For example, if you find an HOA lien on a property, then that's a sign they might be nearing foreclosure. Sure, it's not guaranteed that they're skipping their mortgage payments. Afterall, HOA fees are relatively small and many homeowners consider them less important. Maybe they're just going through hard times and missed a couple months' dues, but still met the mortgage payment every month.

However, if you find an HOA lien and, say, a tax default on the same property, then they're much more likely to be in pre-foreclosure. The taxes are due yearly, and usually taken out of the mortgage escrow.

Now, if you find an HOA lien, tax lien and yet another civil judgment against the homeowner, but still no foreclosure yet, then that's a red-hot pre-foreclosure lead.

Evictions

This is a unique niche that works differently than all the others. By itself, an eviction doesn't tell you anything about the landlord's financial distress or level of motivation to sell. Sure, quite a few of these property owners might be tempted to de-leverage their troubled investment... if the price is right. Which can be difficult for a wholesaler to match and still turn a profit.

The only reason I even include evictions is that there are multiple ways you can profit every time you pick up the phone, even if you never wind up buying the property. Even if this niche isn't your first choice when you're starting out, there are several reasons you'll want to work these leads eventually if you want to scale up:

1) You can generally find the landlord's up to date phone number and address on the eviction notice or rental agreement attached to the eviction complaint. So no skip tracing costs or wasting time with invalid contact info.

2) The sheer volume of these leads ensures plenty of diamonds in the rough. Regardless of the strength of the local housing market, there will always be a steady supply of tenants refusing to pay their rent. In just about every market I have web scrapers for, we see around twice as many fresh evictions every month as new foreclosures and new probate cases combined. This is crucial for scaling, since if you're operating in a smaller market or the local housing scene heats up, you can run out of Tier 1 & Tier 2 leads in a hurry.

3) When you do find a motivated seller in this area, it's often someone who owns multiple properties. Could be mom and pop landlords with a couple of properties they've been managing directly, but now they're looking to cash out and retire. Or a major real estate player with scores of units in their portfolio who needs to liquidate a few assets fast to free up cash for an even bigger deal. In any case, the

increased chances that you'll be able to close multiple deals at once is worth chasing down a few extra dead ends.

4) Even if your acquisition price is much higher than with distressed sellers, these contracts can be sold at a premium price to end buyers. Your investors won't need such a large equity cushion to cover X factors. When you can demonstrate exactly how much rent the current owner has been fetching, you're removing a big unknown risk factor for buyers looking for income producing properties.

And for flippers, they're attracted to the quick turnaround time and low out of pocket cash expenses. While you can expect some damage from the troublesome ex-tenant, the property was usually well-maintained until recently. It's not something that was vacant and neglected for a long time, so the amount of work and time needed to get this asset up to selling standards is relatively miniscule.

5) Referral opportunities without a sale. Obviously, if you have a real estate license, then this niche is solid gold. You can secure endless quick rental listing agreements without ever leaving your office. But even if you're unlicensed, you can still profit directly by referring these leads to agents and property managers for a flat rate fee, or indirectly by gifting them to cash investors to build up goodwill. You're not going to get rich this way, but a steady stream of small referral fees at least covers your marketing and labor costs to work this niche.

6) Even if none of the above work out, you're still on the phone with someone who is a potential cash buyer for your other deals. One of the first questions you can expect when you start talking about their eviction is, "How did you get my number and find out about all of this?" Don't worry though, nine times out of ten they're genuinely curious and not offended.

So now's a perfect time to tell them more about your wholesaling system, ask about their preferred investment style and get their email to send them a sample of what you bring to the table.

Tier 3 – Wildcard leads.

These are the ones that you can identify in court records as fitting all the lead criteria you're looking for or none of them. It all depends on unknown factors that you won't know of until you talk to the seller. You don't want to ignore this class of leads, but you should save them for when you've scaled to the level where you're running low on Tier 1 & 2 prospects.

Open Divorce Cases

This is a classic example of a niche that can be incredibly lucrative or a complete waste of time, depending on the circumstances. The only way to tell what type of situation you're getting into is to pick up the phone and talk to the sellers.

Complicating matters is that, in order to reduce competition, you need to contact divorcing couples as soon as they apply for the dissolution of marriage, and not wait for a public notice to be filed or the divorce to finalize. When you're reaching out so early in the process, there's a good chance the owners haven't yet decided what they want to do with their property.

On the other hand, if they are willing to sell, they're frequently just as motivated as someone in foreclosure, plus they don't have the cloudy title issues. In most cases, they were making their mortgage payments on time, but due to this civil war in their relationship they're now looking to cut living expenses and free up extra cash as soon as possible.

The great wildcard factor here is you're dealing with two different owners of a property, both of which don't exactly see eye to eye. And with the emotions involved, neither one might be acting rationally. What do you do when one person wants to sell and the other refuses, simply out of spite? As a wholesaler, you're not going to have much success assuming a partial interest in the property and then trying to force a partition sale. Few professional investors would be interested, no matter the discount.

So this is a niche that will require more follow up contacts than most. Don't be surprised if the owners are eager to sell on your initial call, but then have second thoughts when you send the paperwork. On the flip side, don't be discouraged if one owner rushes to sign and the other holds out for more money, or even refuses to sell all together. The life situation for both parties is in massive upheaval, so their plans are constantly changing. But as long as you stay in contact and offer tips on how to deal with creditors, you'll be the only buyer that they can trust.

Death & Estate filings without probate

Remember, there's a reason we don't just pull all death certificates and match them to property records. The exact process of property transfer from deceased to heirs varies from state to state, but in most cases you'll find that a surviving spouse or other family member living in the property now holds title.

This does us no good, since we're only looking for motivated sellers that need to sell fast, rather than pestering everyone who has had a death in the family. On the same token though, scanning the probate cases will not identify everyone who has inherited a property that they want to sell.

For example, the probate process is quite expensive, which means not every heir can afford the attorney fees involved. In many jurisdictions, the state offers an expediated and cheaper "summary administration" type of probate procedure (this can go by many names) for estates after a certain amount of time has passed. So, many heirs are just sitting on the property until they qualify for that legal option. The earlier you contact the new owner and offer to purchase the property in cash, and pay the probate attorney fees to boot, the greater the win-win situation you can create for everyone.

In any case, there are a few red flags we can search for that make it likely the new owner is a motivated seller. To consider these Tier 1 leads, you have to invest more time to take a closer look at the case information and see if:

- Does the current owner/rep live in the property? If they're living somewhere else, especially out of state, then you have a potentially motivated seller.

- Is the property listed for rent or was it listed for rent since the owner's passing?

- Were there any guardianships/power of attorney records created for the deceased before they passed? If so, take a look at the grantee and see if the person taking care of the deceased live at the property at the time. If not, then a likely motivated seller.

- Does the property still qualify for homestead tax exemption? If so, why? Who's living there? This approach isn't perfect, because not every county updates the tax exemption when the estate is created, but it is a useful second step to flag motivated sellers.

Request for partition sale

These are the situations where you have multiple owners of a property that can't agree on what to do with it, and at least one party has petitioned the court to force a sale at auction. You'll most often find these after the probate process is complete and more than one heir was granted ownership.

Obviously, this isn't ideal because at least one owner is not just refusing to sell, but also acting irrationally. Barring exceptional circumstances, the partition request will be granted eventually. The only variable being how much of the property's equity gets eaten up by attorney fees. There's just no way they'll earn more from the auction proceeds than they would get from even a wholesale cash deal now.

On the other hand, these people are so drained by their family squabbling, and have often racked up huge legal fees, that if you can get through to them you can shine as an angel investors.

So with this niche, your goal is to share your numbers and make sure every party understands exactly what will happen at auction. There's no guarantee anyone will regain their commonsense, but at least your offer will stand out in comparison to the auction option. You can expect a lot of dead ends here, but at least you won't be looking at much competition.

Bankruptcy

Despite seeming like a no-brainer, this class of leads is not quite as hot as you might expect. If you're willing to spend some extra time searching for specific motions in court cases and sorting through a ton of chaff, then you can still find some ultra-motivated sellers at the right time though.

The first problem is that bankruptcy is often used as a last-ditch effort to avoid foreclosure on a homestead property. If the owner is willing to go to such extremes, then you're looking at pretty much the exact opposite of a motivated seller.

If the bankruptcy doesn't involve a homestead property but rather a second home or investment property, then you might have a chance.

So in this case, you're looking to contact these distressed seller leads not at the beginning of their bankruptcy, but much later. Whenever you see that a "motion of relief from stay" has been granted. You won't be the first investor they've spoken to, but you'll be the first they've talked to since they ran out of options.

But before you start skip tracing (you'll get ultra-low engagement with letters in this niche), research the property involved to make sure they still own it.

Quite often, the bankruptcy action comes so late in the process that the asset has likely already been sold or foreclosed upon. And I mean with a completed foreclosure, where the property has already been auctioned off or is now bank-owned real estate under a listing agreement.

How Should We NOT Source Leads?

Leads from cash buyer websites.

Unless you're running the website yourself, all these supposed "super hot leads" are ice cold. This approach sounds tempting, sure, since the distressed homeowner is actively looking for a quick cash sale, but you aren't going to win the Great Bidding War. Even if you do, it's usually a Pyrrhic victory.

Think about the type of home seller who is proactively reaching out online for quick cash buyers, rather than sticking up a For Sale sign in their yard or hiring a listing agent. Yes, they're obviously motivated, but in just about every case these contacts are a waste of time for wholesalers, since one or more of the following is happening:

- If facing foreclosure, these desperate sellers are likely quite far along in the process. Many people staring down the barrel of that debt cannon get scared and abandon the property as soon as they get the Lis Pendens or notice of sale letter. Those with more stomach get a lawyer and fight the lender, or try to scrounge up the cash to work out a loan modification program with the bank. Or grab a listing agent and sell the property on the open market during the pre/early foreclosure period.

The vast majority only start reaching out to cash buyer websites, or call those homemade bandit signs on the side of the road, once they're in desperate straits. When all legal maneuver options have been exhausted and the auction is imminent. While that might sound great from an investor's perspective, you can bet the seller is being inundated with cash offers.

So in the best-case scenario, you'll wind up in a 50-way bidding war. And that's assuming the owner hasn't already accepted an offer between when you paid for the lead and when you actually got the prospect on the phone. In short, you've come too late to the party. The only exception is if you contacted them previously, in the early or pre-foreclosure phase. Then you've built up a little rapport. I've resurrected many dead leads at the last minute by simply calling them up about two weeks before the auction and asking if I can help. But that only works if you got to them early in the process.

- If the seller is not facing immediate foreclosure, but is under the gun from some other extreme life event, then you are in a bidding war by definition. Since they have a little more flexibility, they can take time to shop around offers. You can bet they've already submitted their contact info to the top 10 "cash for houses in my town" search results on Google. And if it's truly a good deal and investors realize there's more equity involved than usual, every cash buyer will be upping the ante. Sure, I suppose you might get lucky, but luck isn't an investment strategy. That's gambling. If that's your strategy, then go play in a casino. You'll have more fun than in real estate and probably won't lose as much money.

- If the seller is not under serious pressure to sell fast, then they are just window shopping. They're seeing all these cash offer ads and bandit signs everywhere and that's piqued their curiosity, so they dipped their toes in the water to learn more. After being insulted by the first few low ball offers, they now tune out as soon as they hear the word "cash" from any buyer. So you just spent marketing dollars and irreplaceable time chasing down a dead end "lead."

Any pre-made list of leads for sale.

This is where a data broker employs some simple, low-cost web scraping tools to snatch the low hanging fruit. The leads might look great on the outside, but they're far from ripe when you take a bite. Remember that this information isn't fresh, nor vetted to make sure it matches the four criteria of a hot lead. On the backend, the most common techniques data brokers use to generate these leads are:

- Scrapping public notices in newspapers. Such as the notice to creditors to find probate leads or the notice of sale/default with foreclosures. Sure, these represent motivated sellers, but you're learning about them when everyone else does. Guaranteed they've already been contacting by quite a few listing agents, wholesalers and even direct cash investors that can outbid you.

- Crawling tax rolls to find "absentee" landlords. This is a simple search to identify every property that has a mailing address different than the physical address. Sounds great on paper, but doesn't work in practice because you're not honing your marketing like I mentioned previously. At least 90% of these people have no interest in selling their vacation home or investment property, especially not for quick cash at below market rates. Just like with sending out mass mailings to every home in a zip code, you're still spending thousands just to sort through a ton of chaff.

Even when you find someone interested in a sale, they aren't that motived to sell off-market for cash at a discounted price, since they don't have any major financial distress. The best you can hope for with this system is to accidentally stumble upon someone about to face a foreclosure... in which case you can save your money and target only these people from the courthouse records.

- Involuntary liens. Such as Federal and state tax liens, or HOA and hospital liens. Now this might be confusing because these can represent quality pre-foreclosure leads... assuming you find them *before or immediately after the lien is recorded*. Not months or years down the road. To get that head start, you have to scan the open judgments at the local clerk of court's website at least on a weekly basis. You want to know about these things before everyone else, or else where is your edge?

But crawling and parsing court records is hard to do, so a lot of people just wait until the judgment is complete and filed at the land records website. Which is the equivalent of a public notice. That website is usually quite simple to search, even manually without web scrapers, but that's the problem. Because it's so easy, everyone's doing it and you'll be facing much more competition.

Just apply your BS filter to every lead list you're offered. If these leads are so gosh darn awesome, why is anyone selling them? It makes about as much sense as a friend trying to set you up with their ex. If he/she is so hot and just so perfect, then how come you two never talk anymore?

Note: Some of you might be wondering how long my bi-polar personality has gone undiagnosed, since I just spent several pages bashing 3rd party sources of leads and now I'm going to plug my own lead generation service.

The key is that I don't claim to have any unique "insider" knowledge in your local marketplace. In the next chapter I'll show you step by excruciatingly boring step how to look up true leads yourself. My research team simply automates this process and saves you time. Nothing more, but nothing less. You could hire a programmer to build your own scripts, or hire a data entry clerk to manually scan the court records. Either way, you'd get the exact same results as with my service.

My real goal with selling leads is quite simple: I used to run a call center full of agents. But why pay them commissions just to use my tools and work the leads coming from my software? So nowadays when I have clients looking for properties outside of my usual stomping grounds, it's cheaper and faster for me to turn to the network of savvy wholesalers that I've trained and armed with my automation tools, rather than overload my in-house sales team.

So in the interest of full disclosure, let me be clear: this book is intended as a Trojan Horse. The goal is to give you the tools and knowledge to close more deals than you know what to do with, and then you'll come waving high-equity contracts in my face for a simple assignment fee. Win-win for everyone.

Anything you found on Zillow, FSBO, the MLS or similar 3rd party real estate website

This is the junk food you find when Googling "[whatever niche] properties for sale in [my town]." Yes, the property looks pretty tasty, but it's just not healthy for your business to fill up on this crap.

A good example is any website showing you "pre-foreclosure" properties. All they mean is that the property hasn't been sold at auction yet, but it is most definitely in foreclosure. And it has been for months. Maybe years. You will not even be in the top 100 investors that have called, texted or mailed these homeowners.

So don't fall for this trap. Head to the courthouse website to find genuine pre-foreclosures that no one else knows about yet. It'll be quite a research workout, but you'll earn a real treat when you're done.

Anything sourced from public notices.

Just like with the "leads" coming from cash buyer websites, public notices aren't worth your time. It might not seem like that at first. For example, if the public notice doesn't include the property's address and you go the extra step of searching the tax rolls by the deceased's name for the property in question. You might feel like you've done some valuable research, but the lead is still too old for a wholesaler's purposes.

You'll see this with probate/estate leads all the time. For example, when the Notice to Creditors is posted. In most states, this must come X number of weeks before the judge can hold a hearing on the petition for administration. So it sounds like you're coming early to the party. And then you look up the property address on Zillow or the MLS and see it's off-market, so surely you're on to something, right?

In practice though, when you call, the PR is quite jaded and just wants to know your top offer. She's heard all of these cash offer pitches a million times. How did anyone else know? Then you look up the case history at the local courthouse and, holy crap, the petitioner originally filed for probate months ago. Sometimes even years have gone by before the byzantine probate process was far enough along to send out the public notice.

So always go straight to the courthouse source if you want to arrive first to the party.

Online advertising for leads.

You've probably seen the advice to post "we buy houses in cash" on Craigslist, or purchase ads on Facebook. Maybe Google ads to promote your website or whatever the latest marketing fad is. These strategies are tempting because they do work to a certain extent… but not well enough nor often enough to justify the expense for a wholesaler.

Internet ads are just the digital version of mailing a letter to every address in a zip code. For example, maybe a savvy online marketer can help you refine your target audience to roughly approximate folks going through foreclosure in a particular county, but it's never going to be a fraction as accurate as the court records. So a bunch of money wasted showing ads to unmotivated sellers and even more costly time thrown away talking to sellers that are expecting near market rate purchase offers.

Anti-discrimination laws alone limit how specific you can target any housing-related ad. Even if you find a legal way around this and can build an ultra-specific PPC campaign, there's no way to target precisely where in the foreclosure or probate process this homeowner is. You'll be wasting most of your advertising budget getting engagement from folks that are the furthest along in the case and are just shopping around cash offers.

The only way online advertising works on a consistent basis is if you can offer additional services in addition to wholesaling. For example, if you're also a licensed real estate agent, foreclosure defense attorney, run a property management company, credit repair service, etc…

If you're just advertising online for wholesale opportunities, you might score some sales, but the "costs of goods sold" are rarely sustainable in the long run.

How To Source These Off-Market Leads And What To Do With The Data.

At the end of the day, the only sources of truly hot and renewable real estate leads come from either local court records or personal contacts. Networking is way beyond the scope of this book, and it's something that will come naturally anyway as you build up your business and establish your reputation. So I want to focus on the only source of infinite leads that anyone can access right now, regardless of your connections, finances or local market conditions. And that's your boring but oh-so-important local Clerk of Court's website.

Note: If you are in one of those rare jurisdictions that does not have their court records online and requires you to come by in person, then you should really consider investing outside of your county. Especially as a wholesaler who doesn't need an extensive "ground game" to break into a new market. You just need someone to take video and, above all, get as much data as possible. The edge you'll receive from on-demand access to this endless source of high-quality leads far outweighs the inconveniences of investing in a new area.

Now, some details are going to change, depending on what data is available in your marketplace and in general by how you want to run your business. In the beginning, keeping track of everything can be quite a challenge, but it's important not to lose sight of the big picture of what we're doing. At the very minimum, here's our workflow for sourcing leads, screening the information and getting ready to contact sellers, whether you're doing everything yourself or delegating it to an assistant. We'll cover all these steps in detail over the next few chapters, but here's the general workflow:

1. Search local court records by case or document type for new court filings that flag one of the leads we're looking for.

2. Extract the names and addresses of the key stakeholders from each case that you need to contact, such as the landlord, homeowner or divorcing couple.

3. Look up the property in question at your local property appraiser's website and extract the key information you need to screen properties for your end buyers.

4. Put all this information in an Excel spreadsheet to keep it organized.

5. Compare the property details with Zillow to remove any property that's currently for sale.

6. Filter out any property that's underwater (owes more on the judgment than the property is worth) or otherwise doesn't fit your investment criteria.

7. Find comps for the subject and run your CMA.

8. Estimate ARV, your initial offer price and max offer price for each lead. To save time, you can use automated tools for the first screening to get your initial offer, but always run your own CMA, ARV and max price calculations by hand before sending the contract to a seller.

9. Run the remaining point of contact names and addresses through a skip tracing service to get their phone number. If you don't have the resources to call them all, at least call the most valuable ones yourself and don't rely solely on letters.

10. Import this complete file to your CRM software so you can activate your sales process.

Courts we're interested in

While your local court structure will vary drastically from state to state and even county to county inside a state, you want to make sure you're looking for these types of records at the following courts:

- The county-level civil court. Here you'll usually find divorce filings, evictions and lower dollar value foreclosures, like HOA/COA.

- The circuit-level civil court that your county is in. These generally handle the higher value judgments, such as original mortgage (first lien holder) foreclosures.

- The probate or family court for your county. You're only interested in the probate cases that involve real estate though.

- You can generally ignore criminal, traffic, and appeals courts.

- Federal court records usually are not worth your time. It's true that some foreclosures are handled in Federal courts, but they aren't so common and the data is too easy to scrape. You're looking at too much competition.

Depending on your location, these might all be searchable from a single website or might require you to visit multiple sites. If your local court records just aren't available online or they're behind a prohibitively expensive paywall, then check how accessible nearby counties are. The data advantage you gain from having access to these court records far outweighs the inconvenience of having to invest in a new area slightly out of your comfort zone.

If you're in doubt on where to begin, explain to your title attorney the types of records you're looking for and ask them which websites to check. You might have to contact a separate probate attorney as well, since that's a different legal niche.

The specific process for extracting data will also vary across each website. Some strictly forbid the use of automation tools, some make it easy to export data in .CSV format and others might require a fee for bulk data collection.

You might even come across search restrictions, such as not being able to search by date range or must include a name. Don't get discouraged though if you need to hire data entry clerks or a 3rd party data broker service to get what you need. The harder it is to access this information in your marketplace, the fewer people will be doing it and therefore the greater your edge when you work around these issues.

Case or Document types we're looking for

There might be some local differences in the names of documents, so if you don't see a verbatim match here, then just ask your title attorney what court document needs to be filed to start a court case in whichever niche you're looking at.

Whenever possible, make sure you're searching the **open** or **pending** cases/judgments for leads, rather than closed or disposed cases/judgments. Once a case is complete, it'll be recorded at the land records office and a public notice issued, which means you'll be looking at much more competition when you reach out.

- Judicial foreclosures: Lis Pendens. This is the initial notification of a lawsuit. Ignore any foreclosure related searches, because those generally show upcoming auctions. We want to get in on the ground floor, before everyone else knows about this.

- Non-judicial foreclosures: There may not be any court records until the auction is scheduled. In some states though, there is some notice of default or other request for a hearing filed with the courts. This is not the same as any notice of default recorded at the land records office or other public notice of default in the newspaper.

- Probate: Petition for Administration. There are many subtypes of probate administration, and it's not always clear from the metadata which are dealing with real estate. So you might need to read the full petition to find those with estates trying to liquidate real estate. For example, the deceased might still have a property in their name and an open probate case, but when you look at the details the property was passed along through joint tenancy to an heir and the probate case is just seeking to disburse liquid assets, like bank accounts and stocks.

- Evictions: Removal of tenant case or Writ of Possession at the end.

- Divorce: Application for dissolution of marriage. Before the divorce is finished and posted as a public notice.

- Liens & civil judgments: Your county might break them down by type, such as HOA, mechanic's liens, hospital liens, etc... but even if they're all lumped together the data is still useful. You or your assistant can download all the results and sort through them later by plaintiff type or judgment amount.

- Code violations: These are usually recorded as civil judgments, with the city or county as the plaintiff. Even if they are assessed as fines rather than recorded as liens, they'll still need to be satisfied at closing or else the buyer is on the hook for them.

- Bankruptcy: Generally you're looking for Chapter 13 bankruptcies, but successful motions for relief from an automatic stay in Chapter 7 can flag homeowners that have lost their homestead exemption and now have to sell fast.

Property appraiser or Tax assessor website

This website is usually the most universally accessible to the public. You're probably already used to searching it for background on your properties, but there are three other great ways to take advantage of the data here:

- Match the names of leads with properties. Some courthouses don't give full access to the supporting documents in a case, so you're staring at a list of homeowners who just started foreclosure but don't have any of their property addresses. Searching by name is also necessary when you're automating your court records searches.

- Now, there are some states and counties that don't allow you to search the tax rolls by name, such as California, but there are legal ways around that. Contact a data broker, such as my company, for assistance. Or just invest in a different area. It's a big country. Location means little to a wholesaler. It's all about access to data, volume of leads and salesmanship.

- Research building code violations. We'll cover this more in the due diligence section later, but one of the nastiest surprises for wholesalers and end buyers are unlicensed renovations/repairs to a property. However, the best red flag that the homeowners have done work that's going to need inspection and possibly incur fines for the buyer later is if the property data on this site does not exactly match any past listings of the property, what you're hearing over the phone or seeing in person.

- Research your comps. Sourcing your comps from recent, nearby sales at the property appraiser's office gives you the most complete picture of prices in your area. This dataset covers all types of title transfers, including FSBO sales, and not just MLS sales. It also shows you the real final sales price at closing.

- Identify active cash flippers in your area. We'll cover this in detail in the last chapter of this book, but the recent sales data at the appraiser's office is quite useful. You'll be able to spot and get the name/mailing address of active investors who are taking title to distressed properties with a QCD and then selling the same property on the open market a few months later. Exactly the type of experienced cash buyers you want as clients.

Land records/register of deeds

After you've discovered a quality prospect, you need to search the owner's name at your local land records office to see what other liens are on the property. This is an important step for several reasons:

1) When you add up all the property's outstanding debt, you now know the seller's breakeven price before you ever contact them.

2) Knowing how much and to whom they owe money gives you a major knowledge advantage when you contact sellers and helps them trust you more.

3) You can refine your lead list to remove those that have additional mortgages or unpaid assessments that put them underwater. That way you're only reaching out to property owners that can sell their property within your price range.

4) In the foreclosure niche, this is the only way to see where the foreclosing party stands in the lien priority. You'll discover many opportunities to take title cheaply via a QCD or double close, rather than assigning a purchase contract.

Remember this website is for additional research on existing leads. For conducting your due diligence before signing the contract and sending it to your buyer. This isn't the place to research leads in the first place. It might be tempting, since this site is usually much easier to search than the courthouses, but the information is not so fresh. The liens recorded here come after judgments are already closed, so there's a higher chance someone else has reached out to your lead already. Plus, in many counties, the land register takes weeks to update, so the information isn't coming in real time.

Who's who in civil court documents? Untangling Grantor, Grantee, Plaintiff, Defendant, Deceased, Petitioner, Personal Rep, etc...

Obviously, it's great when your local courthouse allows unfettered access to the full complaint and all the case details, but every county is different. In some cases, you might only be able to read the bare-bones court docket information, which simply names the case type and parties involved. But that's still enough information to find out what property is likely available for sale and who you should contact:

- Judicial Foreclosures, Pending Judgments, and Recently Filed Involuntary Liens: **Grantee/defendant** is the potential seller to contact and title holder to look up the property address. In first lien holder foreclosures, there will likely be multiple defendants. Usually the first defendant listed is the debtor, but if you're unsure, read the details of the complaint to find the mortgage holder's name.

- Non-Judicial Foreclosure Notices of Default: **Grantor/Trustor** is the homeowner facing foreclosure.

- Evictions: **Plaintiff** is the landlord to contact. The plaintiff listed on the metadata might only be the attorney or property management company, so it's often necessary to read the complaint and get the landlord's actual name and contact info from the lease agreement/Notice of Eviction.

- Probates: The title is still held in the Decedent's name, but the **Petitioner/Personal Representative** is the person to contact to purchase the property.

- Divorces: Contact both parties, but you'll have to double check the property appraiser's data to see if both names are listed on the title. For example, if this is a non-homestead property, only one spouse might be on the deed.

Priority of Liens

Some wholesalers skim over the details about how to evaluate liens on a property. And while some of the strategies I'll mention here aren't applicable to a wholesale-by-assignment-only business, you'll still gain a huge advantage if you understand the big picture of how these liens affect you, the seller and the end buyer.

Here's the ten-second primer if you're brand new to real estate: Liens, whether voluntary (ex. a mortgage) or involuntary (ex. unpaid taxes), represent interest stakes in a property... but all interests are not created equal. There's a priority system to determine who gets paid first, second, third, etc... at a foreclosure auction. The general rule of the thumb is the "first in time, first in right" principle. Meaning that the first lien recorded on a property needs to be fully satisfied when the asset is sold before the second lien receives any payment and so on.

Now, in a regular sale, all liens have to be paid in full to transfer the title. That's why it's so important for a wholesaler to check the lien history on a property. Liens can only be cleared in one of three ways:

1. By satisfying the full amount at closing, during a regular sale.
2. By taking title through a quit claim deed and negotiating lower settlements with creditors prior to a regular sale.
3. After an auction sale, although this won't eliminate government liens.

How to make liens work in your favor.

First, simply taking a few extra minutes to screen for this debt ahead of time will guarantee your equity estimate will be much more accurate and make sure you don't overpay for the property. That already puts you ahead of the game, since most investors wait until right before closing to get blindsided by the title report, but we can take things a bit further.

For classic wholesaling: Educate the homeowner about how deep in debt they really are. They might know exactly how much they owe the first mortgage lender, but are they factoring in what they have to pay in their HELOC loan from another bank? Or from the back taxes and unpaid HOA fees? Or the unpaid sewer/water bill that's become a lien on their property? The list of potential creditors snatching an interest stake in their property goes on and on.

Many owners have trouble seeing how all these liens and fines add up into the big debt picture and overestimate the equity they have in their home. In some cases, they might not even know about a lien or think a debt is personal and not tied to the property. So you can blow their minds and really stand out from the pack by showing them your research when negotiating price.

Remember, you're an angel investor. So you want to focus the narrative on what you're saving them from. For example, they aren't giving up $70k in equity when they sell a $200k house for $130k. Instead, focus on how you're taking $120k in credit-destroying debt off their shoulders. And then tossing in $10k in cash to boot.

Regarding fast flips that aren't really wholesaling, but you'll be tempted to work on soon:

Understanding the priority of liens helps you negotiate a lower payoff to unlock more equity. Similar to the concept of a short sale, but even easier, you can contact the secondary lien holders and offer a lump sum payment for part of the amount owed. This is especially lucrative in states that allow the forecloser to seek additional judgments beyond the outstanding balance, such as for attorney fees. The secondary lien holders know the odds are slim that anything will be left over for them if the property goes to auction, so they're much more inclined to settle for anything they can get now.

When you purchase a property at a foreclosure auction (or sheriff sale), whether the forecloser is a lender, tax authority or HOA, this is still important. You need to know which liens will survive the process and which liens will be entitled to the auction surplus. Your final title search will spell out exactly what you need to do to gain clear title, but obviously you want to know this information before you even bid on a property so you can position yourself ahead of time.

- If you know which weaker interests will be wiped out in the auction, such as mechanic/contractor liens, you can adjust your equity estimate to bid a little higher for the property. This gives you an edge over other investors who, in a rush in these time-limited auctions, just tally up all the debt listed publicly on the property records.

Just to clarify, since I'm talking about different strategies at once: Liens can only be eliminated through an auction foreclosure by a superior lender. That's the beautiful thing about buying at auction. The 1st lien holder is doing the heavy lifting and wiping out other debt, so they're creating equity out of thin air. You still need to know about all these liens in a regular wholesale deal though, since your purchase price must be high enough to satisfy them all at closing in order to clear title.

- If you've found hidden debt that's not yet recorded on the property records, you can adjust your bid accordingly to make sure you don't overpay.

- You'll also be amazed how often a lien has been paid off and satisfied, but for one reason or another the lien release has not been recorded. You'll find this most often with older probate homes or properties that have had multiple sales in the last few years. And of course, in super lien states, there are plenty of people who pay off the HOA lien *after* the lender has foreclosed, which is free money for you.

- In some cases, you might find that the foreclosing lien holder's judgment is quite small in comparison to the property's market value. This would leave a very large surplus in the sale. If there are no other lien holders, or their interest priority is lower than yours, you could just make sure you have an ironclad rights assignment from the homeowner, HOA or whomever you purchased interest from and let the property go to auction. Then you can profit from the surplus without spending any time or money rehabbing the property.

Liens that almost always survive foreclosure:

- Federal Tax Liens issued by the IRS or other rare Federal agencies, like the Department of Justice or Treasury. If the government does not exercise its redemption right within 120 days after the sale, the lien will expire.

- State, county and city tax liens.

- Code enforcement and zoning violations.

Liens that usually survive foreclosure, but state specific:

- Demolition or environmental based liens.

- State child support lien (not wage garnishments).

- Special assessments for local infrastructure.

- Government utility liens and delinquencies not recorded as liens, such as sewer/water.

- Judgment liens, such as damages awarded in a lawsuit.

Liens usually wiped out in foreclosure, if the lien holders were properly notified of their right to bid on the property at auction:

- Second, reverse and other later mortgages, home equity loans and lines of credit.

- Credit card judgments recorded after the forecloser's lien.

- Personal judgments recorded after the forecloser's lien.

- Mechanic's liens recorded after the forecloser's lien.

- Most non-government entity liens filed after the forecloser's lien.

- HOA/COA liens. However, in some "super lien" states, part or all of the unpaid HOA/COA liens can take precedence over the original lender and be paid off first.

General Overview Of The Foreclosure Process And Opportunities

Note: Depending on your real estate experience level, this section might be remedial, and not all of these strategies are applicable to wholesaling by assignment, but I'm including this background info for the sake of thoroughness.

Since you're not going to find significant equity in homes already for sale on the market, then we will be dealing with properties that are at some stage of the pre-foreclosure process. You don't have to be a foreclosure specialist at the beginning to take advantage of the system, although you will reach that skill level faster than you might think. In the meantime, lean on your attorney to cover all the legal minutia. Make them earn their keep.

Right now, you just need to focus on mastering the "big picture" of how all these moving parts fit together and where you can step in to add value. In the next phase we'll bring all these strategies together in step by step practice.

There are two main types of lender-originated foreclosures, but both lead to the same goal of selling the home to pay off the outstanding debt, the vast majority of the time through a public auction. Now, I focus the most attention on judicial foreclosures throughout this book, since they offer several unique advantages for investors. Still, most of these strategies, tips, tricks, as well as notes of caution, can be applied to evaluate equity, unlock new value and gain a competitive advantage in non-judicial foreclosures.

Now, the state you're operating in does play a major role on your investment strategy. Not your success or failure rate, of course not, but how aggressively you should pursue certain options. For example, Florida requires that all foreclosures must be judicial, where the lender sues the borrower to go to auction. In this case, gaining title from the homeowner and then delaying the sale while you flip the property or earn a rental income in the meantime are fairly simple and lucrative strategies.

On the other hand, California requires that all foreclosures be non-judicial, where the lender can go straight to auction by following a public notice procedure. Since it's harder and more expensive to delay a sale there, it's usually a better strategy to focus on negotiating cash-for-keys settlements with the lender or positioning yourself as the surplus holder when the property goes to auction so you have bidding leverage.

Complicating things further, many states allow both foreclosure types without mandating one or the other, letting the borrower and lender decide the terms of the mortgage contract. Quite often this includes adding special failure to pay provisions to the contract, which may or may not even hold up in court. *Sigh*. I know, but I warned you'd be spending a ton of time talking to your lawyer. Don't worry though. When you understand the broad strokes and the opportunities available with each foreclosure, you'll know exactly what questions to ask your attorney. That alone puts you way ahead of most of your competitors.

Types of Foreclosures by State

There's no way for this book to stay abreast of every single state's foreclosure laws, so you simply have to ask your attorney how things are handled in your particular market.

1) Some states allow only judicial foreclosures. Where the creditor has to sue the debtor to foreclose. From a purely data-availability perspective, these are the markets a wholesaler will have the largest advantage in.

2) A smaller number of states allow only statutory foreclosures/trustee sales, which will make it much harder to get a head start over other investors. You'll have to do more research in the court records to identify likely pre-foreclosures by secondary indicators, such as for unpaid taxes and outstanding HOA assessments.

3) The majority of states technically allow both types of foreclosures, although you'll generally find that trustee sales that don't involve the courts are far more common. The number of mortgages subject to a judicial foreclosure will likely vary wildly from city to city. Lenders want to go through the streamlined statutory foreclosure process whenever possible, so it's only local laws or heavy

competition in the local credit market that can force them to offer debtor-friendly foreclosure clauses.

Judicial Foreclosure

This is where the mortgage owner files a civil lawsuit against the original borrower to recover the unpaid debt by forcing a sale of the property. There are procedural differences in each state, such as length of redemption periods, time between notices and extra paperwork, but the general process works like this:

1) *Notice.* After at least four months of missed payments, the lender files a Lis Pendens (generic notice of lawsuit) at the county or circuit courthouse where the property is located. This is all a matter of public record, since it serves to warn perspective buyers that the property's title is disputed and to protect the lender's interest until the lawsuit (foreclosure) is resolved.

   For our purposes, web scraping every incoming lawsuit is the first step in our lead generation process. This Lis Pendens rarely includes any other information besides the names of the parties involved. You'll have to check the associated case number and often read the complaint itself to find the default date and amount owed. But it's all worth it to estimate equity so we can see if the property is worth pursuing and how low we can go in our initial offer.

   The most important thing is data mining the Lis Pendens records before a final judgment has been issued by the court gives us a big head start over everyone else. We can now estimate with close accuracy the total payoff debt load and the home's value, thus giving us a firm estimate of how much equity is in the property. Then we screen the list for the best deals and track down the owners before every other investor jumps on the distressed homeowner.

2) *Judgment.* Weeks to years later, depending on how savvy the defendant's lawyer is, the local court then decides a final judgment amount for the lender, which includes the outstanding loan balance, plus late fees, interest and attorney fees. This is the amount the lender is entitled to collect from the property's auction sale. The owner has many legal options to delay this judgment, but the longer it takes the higher the judgement amount will be and the more equity gets eaten up by the lender.

Now we're at the point when competition for the property really heats up. Instead of estimating equity, so many cash investors will wait until the final judgement is posted publicly before approaching the homeowner in a distressed sale. Hence why data mining, estimating equity and contacting the owner as early as possible are so important. If you haven't already closed a deal to take title from the homeowner by now, it's likely time to move on. The phone is going to be busy every time you call and any fliers you send out will get lost in the mountain of tacky cash-offer post cards bulging out of their mailbox.

Note: In some jurisdictions, the lender won't receive a judgment amount and needs to sue the debtor separately after the foreclosure. So in this case, instead of a judgment right now, the court will just grant the plaintiff the right to auction the property.

3) *Sale.* In most judicial foreclosure states, the lender must put the property up for public auction within a certain time frame, usually around three months, after receiving their judgment. Nowadays, these are mostly done online through the local county's courthouse. There are minor variations in auction methods among the 3,000+ counties nationwide, but the key aspects are universal.

The lender will make the opening bid, which may be public or hidden (a blind auction).

If the final auction sales price is higher than the lender's judgment, then any proceeds over that amount (called the surplus) are distributed to other interested parties through the priority of liens system. While there are some "super lien" exceptions from state to state, generally this means anything left over after paying off the first mortgage owner goes to each lien holder in the chronological order their lien was recorded. If there is anything left over, the surplus goes to the homeowner, or to an investor that purchased the homeowner's "rights to surplus" during a QCD title transfer.

If you win the auction, you'll have to make an X% of your bid deposit immediately. You'll only have a small window of time, usually less than 24 hours, to finish your due diligence on the property and make final payment or forfeit your deposit.

Note: While rare, a handful of states, such as Delaware, use a so-called "strict foreclosure" process. Instead of an auction, the court sets a final redemption date a few months in the future. If the defendant (homeowner) does not settle the mortgage by then, the court awards full ownership of the home to the plaintiff (mortgage holder). Much like a repossession. At this point, the home becomes a Real Estate Owned (REO) property that will be put up on the MLS for sale at market rates.

4) *Redemption.* In most states, if the homeowner hasn't paid off or settled the debt before the auction begins, then they're out of luck. Since their interest in the property has been wiped out, if they're still living in the place, they'll be evicted by the new owner. However, a few states allow an additional redemption period after the final sale. This redemption period hold prevents the new owner from assuming full title and reselling the property for a time, sometimes as short as a few days or even as long as six months.

Opportunities and Challenges

In judicial states, it's easy to fight and delay foreclosures, which gives us an additional angle to help the homeowner and build rapport. But remember, barring exceptional circumstances, the lender will win in the end. And in the meantime, the equity is getting eaten up by legal fees.

Which we're going to turn to our advantage when negotiating with sellers, by pointing out that once foreclosure has begun, the price any investor can offer will only go down. Every day they delay means more in attorney fees and back interest to pay off, so the value of the deal will only keep dropping. Still, even if the prospect is refusing to sell now and wants to keep fighting, it's worthwhile to stay in touch and help however you can.

Monitor the case and touch base with them again after one of their motions gets denied. And if you're willing to take title through a QCD, there are many more ways you can profit:

1) In every state, the homeowner can stop foreclosure at any time before the sale by paying off their default amount and bringing their account current, or by settling the final judgement amount if one has been issued.

   This is where angel investors like yourself come into play, as long as you reach the owner fast. You can gain title cheaply from the homeowner, then either quickly put the house up for sale and pay off the debt with the new buyer's funds, or negotiate a short payoff or cash-for-keys arrangement directly with the lender.

   Either way, you're gaining early access to a property before it gets to market, which allows you to turn most of the equity that would otherwise be wiped out at auction into cash in your pocket. For the homeowner, you're taking away the soul-crushing stress and credit destruction that comes with foreclosure away, while turning their debt into a chunk of cash in their pocket. For the lender, they're gaining a quick payoff without having to go through the expense, hassle and risk of foreclosing. A win-win-win scenario across the board.

2) Unfortunately, not everyone thinks so rationally. Some folks will always see business as a zero-sum game, filled with only winners or losers. Or maybe their hands are really tied, such as if you're dealing with a multi-million-dollar property mortgaged by a small non-bank lender. The lone claims agent, who also doubles as the CEO of the lending company, keeps getting an earful from his investors threatening to jump ship and put him out of business if he settles for one cent less than the final judgement. So in this case, I'm going to do him a favor and help him show his investors how much they're losing by being so obstinate. If nothing else, the lender's lawyer is going to love me for helping them buy a new BMW.

If for some reason the lender doesn't want to cooperate and work out a mutually beneficial arrangement, then this judicial process affords you abundant chances to fight the foreclosure. Your legal position is quite strong. You used a quitclaim deed to gain all the homeowner's interest and rights to the property, including the right to litigate on their behalf.

This all makes you a party with indispensable interest in the property, who's not named on the original Lis Pendens. By the way, you'll be surprised how long it takes many lenders to update the lawsuit to even include you. Just one of the countless little mistakes they make that you can leverage into many more months of delay. Also, you never signed any promissory note. They don't have one scrap of paper with your signature on it. In fact, can they produce every single disclosure form and supporting document dating back to the loan's origination, including from all the mortgage servicers it has passed through? Can the plaintiff prove they have the legal right to foreclose and haven't violated any consumer protection laws in the process?

Afterall, this is a *judicial* proceeding first and foremost. They're the plaintiff claiming damages, so the burden of proof rests with them. And best of all, in a legal war of attrition, you have the cost-effectiveness edge here. The minutia of the strategy can get rather complex, but the weapons you're firing are relatively simple and cheap forms, just filed at the right time and in a particular order. Every salvo in this exchange costs you only a fraction as much as the plaintiff in attorney fees, since you're paying only for document prep and filing, while they have to spend many more hours chasing down records and responding.

With the right motion filing strategy, you can delay the sale for several years. At the moment, my longest defensive position in a judicial foreclosure is just under six years old, with no end in sight. In the meantime, you can do what I'm doing. Rent out the property at a generous profit, since your overhead is next to nothing, while putting more pressure on the lender to come to the bargaining table.

3) Well, that was fun while it lasted but all good things must come to an end. Your last motion was denied, an auction date has been set and the judge threatened you with bodily harm if you waste any more of their time with this nonsense. *C'est la vie.*

Actually, the fun is just getting started. When you do finally go to auction, remember that you've taken over the homeowner's interest. Which means you'll be entitled to any surplus at the auction. So you could potentially sit back and profit handsomely even while having your interest stripped away.

Or maybe there's still enough equity left over to make the investment worth your while. So use your position to vastly outbid everyone else and buy the property, since any amount over the judgement will be returned to you. Granted, the legal details are a bit involved and vary state to state. That's why it's crucial to check with your lawyer and make sure you're doing everything right in your local jurisdiction, but that's a snapshot of the profitable fun you can have with judicial foreclosures.

Non-Judicial or Statutory Foreclosure

This is the streamlined foreclosure approach that lets the lender bypass the courts and bring the property straight to auction. It's quite common in some of the hottest real estate markets, such as Arizona, California, Nevada, Texas and Washington. There are many procedural differences across states, but in broad strokes the process follows a simple action flow of: A) notify B) advertise and C) auction:

1) *Notice.* After at least four months in default, the lender issues a Notice of Default to the borrower, which in many states is also recorded in the public records. We can data mine these records and generate our leads from them just as if they were a Lis Pendens in a judicial proceeding. But realize that since everyone can see these at the same time, there will be a lot more competition in non-judicial foreclosure states.

    Because many of these non-judicial states do not allow deficiency judgments, or only allow them later in the foreclosure under certain conditions, this initial notice of default is enough for anyone to calculate equity. You won't have the head start over other cash investors like you would when studying the Lis Pendens for judicial foreclosures, so putting your data to use smarter and faster than everyone else is the key.

Since we're in a race to get these distressed homeowners on the line before the cash investors start a bidding war, here's where the automation, skip tracing and contact strategies we'll cover soon really pay off.

2) *Notice of Trustee Sale*. In some states, the lender can jump straight into scheduling the auction without court involvement. In a few jurisdictions, the forecloser needs some final authorization from the court and you might be able to find that document. In any case, there's a short window of time where the trustee has to advertise the auction. So regardless of when you found these leads, the clock's ticking to close on the deal.

3) *Auction*. This part works just like public auctions in judicial proceedings, with the same priority of liens schedule and bidding process. The primary difference is that since many lenders won't have an inflated deficiency judgment, they're more likely to set their initial bid quite high.

Opportunities and Challenges

We'll still follow the same general strategies as in judicial proceedings, it's just that there's less room for error because the competition is more intense.

On the plus side, these statutory foreclosures often have much more equity in them, since we're not talking about potentially years of back interest and attorney fees tacked onto the default amount. On the other hand, everyone learns that information at the same time, so don't be surprised if the owner accepts your offer verbally, but then calls you back to shop around someone else's deal before you can send the paperwork. Still, if you follow the details in this book and online course, you'll have an edge in these negotiations. Unlike the other investors, you won't be following some seriously flawed value/equity guesses. You'll be able to draw a much finer line between equity and your maximum allowable offer and turn a major profit despite the higher acquisition costs.

The homeowner also still has legal recourse to fight and delay the foreclosure, though this is a bit more complicated. Instead of defending themselves, as with judicial foreclosures, they'll have to sue the lender and seek a temporary restraining order or even injunction to halt the foreclosure. This is totally different than judicial foreclosure delay strategies, since you're asking for an immediate decision from the court rather than trying to postpone a decision as long as possible.

You'll have to talk to a local foreclosure defense attorney to find out useful info for the homeowner, but there's usually something that can be done. These non-judicial foreclosures only allow the lender to bypass the courts if they jump through several hoops. You might be surprised how often you can spot a procedural violation that gives the owner a strong legal case to at least get a temporary restraining order.

This is especially useful if you're interested in doing a QCD title transfer. Once you've thrown off the lender's plans for a quick auction sell and added more red ink to their ledger, they tend to become a little more flexible when you approach them for a short payoff deal. In either case, you'll definitely need a strong foreclosure litigation attorney on your team.

Regardless of whether you're working on a judicial or non-judicial foreclosure, remember that only the loans are being foreclosed upon, and the property is just the collateral. Which means it's possible to have more than one foreclosure going on simultaneously, each at a different phase of the process. You can even have separate judicial and statutory foreclosures occurring at once. So it's important to keep up regular searches for any other court actions started against the seller, even after you sign the purchase agreement.

Using Quit Claim Deeds To Purchase Off-Market Properties:

When you're just starting out with wholesaling, naturally you're going to want to use a standard residential "as is" purchase contract. Then assign that contract within 24 hours for a flat fee. Part of your fee is paid as a non-refundable deposit when you assign, and the rest upon the final closing. The end result is that the buyer receives a general warranty deed from the seller, and backed up by title insurance from the title company.

This is the exact same process you would use if you were making an offer on a house listed for sale on Zillow or the MLS, except that you're purchasing "as is," so the seller doesn't have to fix anything or credit you for any problem.

But this isn't the only way to purchase real estate. Just the easiest. Even if you can't imagine taking on any other risk right now, within a few weeks you're going to get sick and tired of all the missed opportunities with this approach.

You'll see so many opportunities where you could get a much better price or negotiate with creditors if you were taking title directly, instead of providing a regular purchase contract that has to cover all the debt first.

Until you're ready to take advantage of these leads, you're probably just giving them away as freebies to build goodwill with your cash buyers. So it helps to have a general understanding what they're doing with them.

The direct investor is going to the homeowner and getting them to sign a quit claim deed to cede their interest in the property, and all the rights (such as to the auction surplus, with a side agreement that might even include leasing the property back to the seller. All in exchange for a relatively modest payment.

Of course, this is a "dirty" title, which means the investor is going to be responsible for paying off all the debt on the property. Maybe not legally, but they will have to in order to recover their investment.

Advantages of purchasing with Quit Claim Deeds:

1. You need very little upfront cash to pay the owner for the QCD and take title to the property.

2. If the loan is assumable, for example FHA/VA mortgages, then you can offer to take over payments and only shell out of pocket

costs to cover any secondary lien holders. Like a pending HOA foreclosure.

3. If the owner refuses to move, then you can take title cheaply and lease the property back to them.

4. By taking advantage of the priority of liens and haggling with creditors, you can reduce and in some cases even eliminate debt on the property. So you're creating equity out of thin air.

For a common example, say the investor spots an HOA foreclosure that began before the original mortgage holder has started foreclosure. If they move fast, the investor can get the owner to sign over title, then pay off the HOA assessment to stop that foreclosure. Now they're a party with indispensable interest in the property, but no financial obligations when the first lender comes a suin'. Gives the new owner quite an upper hand in negotiating a lower payoff with the lender to avoid years of legal fees.

5. These opportunities are the most bountiful in every market, so you can pick and choose only those with the greatest profit potential to target.

Disadvantages:

1. Risk is multiplied with a dirty title, since you have new liabilities that need to be settled before you can resell the property.

2. Depending on how many liens are on the property and other legal factors, it can take months, in some cases even years, to clear title and flip the property.

3. You usually can't borrow against the value of assets you gathered this way, since the title is cloudy.

Assigning Contracts Versus Double Closing

In this book, we'll focus on the most common form of wholesaling real estate: by assignment. Basically, that's what everyone wants to do, so I'm trying to make it as low stress and risk free as possible. Although all the lessons about finding, screening and closing with leads, as well as finding, vetting and negotiating with end buyers is exactly the same for double closings.

If you plan to actually take title to the property for any period of time, either through a regular sale or via a quit claim deed, and then resell it later, then all that falls under the umbrella of flipping. Which is a wonderful niche, but entails a bit more risk and a different equity evaluation strategy.

However, if you have the money or can secure transactional funding, then double closing offers several huge advantages over assigning contracts.

1) You can earn a lot more, even with the additional closing costs. If you are able to secure a sizeable discount from the seller and have sufficient funds to cover that contract, then double closing can drastically increase your profits. For example, if you locked down a property worth $150k for $75k, the end buyer would be happy to pay you $25k in assignment fees, since they're still walking away with more than 30% equity.

However, you can bet the homeowner is going to be enraged when they see the details of the contract and how much you're making. Hopefully they will only ghost your calls and won't show up at your office with pitchforks and torches. Sure, many truly desperate sellers won't care what you're earning, but those that own quality property that doesn't need vast rehab are not going to be happy.

The most you could reasonably collect through assignment in this situation is around ~$5k before the seller starts having second thoughts. I know I keep harping on this being a high-volume business and not to chase every penny, but we're only human. Leaving $20k on the table for the end buyer to enjoy is a hard pill to swallow.

2) You'll get more interest from end buyers. Obviously, a wholesaler willing to put some skin in the game is going to attract more attention from end buyers. Not only does this help you close more deals and do so faster, but any time there's competition for a property then you have more bargaining power.

3) More advertising options. Now as a buyer with equitable interest in the property, in most jurisdictions all those advertising restrictions

about practicing real estate without a license are removed. You might even be able to attract regular "open market" buyers, if the property just needs staging and light rehab.

4) Quite often, double closing releases your funds even faster than assignment. Since you're closing the purchase and sale on the same day, your proceeds are generally available to reinvest within five business days.

Phase II – Nuts and Bolts of Building a Professional Wholesaling Operation from Scratch

In all honesty, this section probably deserves a full book all on its own. This subject is something we cover in great depth in my online coaching course, since it's really an ongoing process. Still, here are the core fundamentals to get your "backend" sales infrastructure up and running within a week and on a budget. You can refine and perfect things as you scale, but here are the bare-bones minimum tools, resources and processes you should have in place before you ever call your first lead.

And while all of this might seem like common sense, you'll be surprised how few wholesalers bother setting up a well-organized and professional business.

Setting Up Your Outreach Program And Sales Backend.

Don't put off your LLC filing

Yes, most new wholesalers understand that they need to incorporate a limited liability corporation, but consider this a low priority. Something they'll get to one day "once the money is rolling in." What they're missing is that incorporating your sole proprietorship right now will help bring in the money.

Besides the sizeable tax advantages of owning a pass-through company, your company name and logo will lend credibility when you contact sellers. Anything that helps keep them on the phone a few seconds longer or reading another line in your letter will increase your conversion.

And don't forget that the tiny filing fees to set up an LLC are nothing compared to the liability protection you're receiving. It's a classic example of an ounce of prevention being worth a pound of cure.

Finding the right closing agent

Even if the end buyer insists on using their own closing agent, you'll need a "wholesaler friendly" closing agent to prep your paperwork, handle escrow and advise you on all sorts of legal minutia. Plus, soon you'll be closing on deals yourself, either by double closing or direct investing. So I want to take a moment to stress how important it is to vet your closing agent. You're asking for trouble if you just pick the cheapest title attorney that shows up in a Google search.

Yes, all closing agents do the exact thing same thing on paper... but in practice they tend to specialize just like any other profession. So you want one who is used to working with wholesalers and has proven experience handling off-market transactions. This is especially important if you're working leads that are still in probate and require court approval for the sale.

Now, every attorney will say that none of this is a problem and all routine stuff for them. And technically it is, but just because they learned about something in law school doesn't mean they've actually done it recently. For example, maybe they've handled closing for thousands of MLS sales, but never one that was in probate. Then they forget to check a box on one of the court forms, which winds up delaying things by weeks.

So really spell out exactly what you're doing, from start to finish. Explain how you source your leads and that many of them will be in foreclosure at the time of purchase. Make it clear that you won't be the end buyer and plan to assign everything. If you're investing remotely into a new market that you don't live in, explain that you'll be using an online service (like DocuSign) to sign the paperwork and you won't even be physically present at closing.

At this point, an experienced closing agent will understand that this is more complicated than a traditional house flip and will have a bunch of questions for you, just to make sure you understand what you're doing. If they just nod along and say, "No problem," then they probably don't understand all the ins and outs.

Skip Tracing

If you're not familiar with using a 3rd party service to gather phone numbers from just a name and address, this is a perfectly legal and absolutely vital tool in real estate sales. Especially when you're dealing with distressed properties. Let's be honest, odds are someone so deeply in debt is pretty used to ignoring their mail. If you want high engagement, you need to call them.

Now, snail mail will still always play a role in your outreach. Even the best skip tracing reports can't find the right phone number ~25% of the time. I'm just saying at least try to find the number of your hottest leads and don't rely solely on mailings.

There are a million companies offering this service. I recommend LexisNexus. It's a bit more expensive than others, but has a relatively high accuracy rate, which saves you money in the long run.

Find quality virtual assistants

If you're doing this full-time, you're obviously going to be generating more leads than there are hours in the day to follow up with them. You're going to have to bring on an assistant or even a few if you want to get dozens of deals in the pipeline all at once.

If you're wholesaling part-time, then assistants are even more important. Someone needs to be manning the phone and website chat widget while you're at your day job. The last thing in the world you want to do is put in the effort to contact a seller, get their interest, but then have them turn to some other wholesaler because you didn't answer their call immediately.

Remember though, anyone doing the initial telephone outreach or responding to follow up questions from prospects isn't really doing a traditional sales job. They're giving and gathering information, while trying to establish a human connection with the seller.

You can use assistants to make the initial outreach and find out if the homeowner is interested in selling within or near your price range (qualifying), gather information on the property, give the seller general foreclosure/probate advice, make the soft sale pitch (staging) and schedule appointments. In short, all the prep work to warm up the lead, but you're going to handle the final "hard sell," where you negotiate brass tacks and finalize the contract terms, yourself.

That's why, in my experience, it's best to hire assistants with a customer service background, rather than experienced with traditional real estate cold calling.

For example, someone who has worked in face to face retail customer service likely has the empathy, patience, self-confidence and creative troubleshooting skills that you're looking for. They may take a little bit longer to train up, but it's far easier to teach them real estate terminology than it is to teach a jaded cold caller human compassion and mental flexibility. Well, that might be unfairly harsh. I have worked with some great cold callers, but the average person with a "call center" mentality that sticks religiously to the call script will need a lot of micro-management and coaching until they begin adding real value to your business.

Note about compensation: without a real estate license, your assistants can not earn a commission. There may even be other restrictions in your local jurisdiction about what they can and cannot say over the phone, or whether they can earn referral/bounty fees. So again, ask your attorney about what local laws apply not just to you, but your assistants as well.

Field Rep to take on-site video

It's not necessary to see a property before you sign the purchase agreement. In fact, it can even be counterproductive. For example, what if the out-of-town seller is ready to accept your initial offer on Monday, but can't get someone to show you the place until the weekend? Are you really going to sit on this hot lead all week and give someone else the chance to swoop in and sign the owner first?

You've baked in enough equity in your offer to cover common rehab, with a significant margin of error. If the in-person walkthrough uncovers any deal-breaking problems, then that's what the inspection period contingency is for. So never let a physical visit to the property get in the way of securing the contract first.

With that said, after you secure the contract you need to get someone onsite ASAP. Even if they can only film the exterior and not get inside yet. If you plan on assigning this investment fast, without haggling for days, then you absolutely must have a video walkthrough of the property. Pictures alone are simply not enough to get the fast engagement from buyers that we're looking for.

Ideally, this will be done by your in-house listing agent, but when you're just starting out you'll probably be relying on part-time, unprofessional labor. And that's fine, as long as you give them an extremely detailed list of what you want to see on film.

Remember, the video is both a marketing tool for end buyers and a "remote inspection" to back up the claims you're making in your property prospectus. So your field rep needs to run through the standard property inspection checklist, while filming each step of the process. For the sake of brevity, you can start the video with a 2-5 minute high-level tour, where they first walk around the property, then enter it and give a panorama view of each room, including the floor and ceiling. Then you can take as long as you need to film the mundane details of checking the lights, appliances, windows, doors, zooming in on drywall cracks, etc...

Website

You absolutely need to set up a simple cash buyer website to build a casual sales funnel. This doesn't have to be complicated nor extensive though. A simple one-page website with an embedded chat widget is more than enough to get started. And you don't need to invest money into SEO, ads and all that stuff to get online attention.

Random leads stumbling across you on the internet tend to be more trouble than they're worth. You already have an endless source of fresh, high-quality leads. You don't want to waste your time with people who are just shopping for the best cash offer.

The primary purpose of the page is to provide a casual way for the people you've been contacting via mail, email, text or voicemail to engage with you.

If you just contact sellers and say call me back, your engagement will be limited because you're adding a barrier to communications. Lots of people are uncomfortable with calling back a total stranger and need a warmup first. If they can visit your website, see a visual representation of the process and ask questions via the chat widget, they'll be far more likely to schedule a call. A classic sales funnel.

As a bonus, you can also use the website to A/B split test your outreach. For example, you can add a different landing page for each version of your initial contact script and track the stats to see which is resonating best with sellers.

You can grab a pre-made website them and hire a cheap graphic artist on Upwork to make your logo or any other graphics. I know it's a bunch of annoying little things to work on first, but this is stuff you'll only have to do one time and it does pay off down the road.

CRM

A lot of wholesalers consider CRM software a "nice to have" luxury rather than a business-critical expense. I can't stress enough have useful this software is to stay organized, and how crucial staying organized is to your lasting success.

When you send out letters, texts or leave voicemails for hundreds of leads at once, what are you going to do when they call you back? The CRM gives you several advantages over your competitors:

1) You'll know exactly who you're talking to and about what property as soon as you answer the phone. That helps build instant rapport. The typical wholesaler answers a call back by asking a whole

bunch of questions like, "Who is this? What property are you talking about?" Which just leaves a sour taste in the home seller's mouth. After all, you contacted them first. They're taking time out of their day to return your call.

Contrast that to the far more personal response you can give when all the lead's information is at your fingertips. "Oh, Mrs. So and So. Thanks so much for answering my voicemail/text message/letter. I've been looking forward to purchasing your condo at 511 Ocean Beach drive…"

It might sound like such a small detail, but the details will make or break you in this business. The smallest thing you can do to simplify the sales process and make it easier for clients to work with you rather than someone else will always pay handsome dividends.

Even if you're just wholesaling part-time and only trying to work one deal a month, you'll still be balancing a vast network of leads and potential buyers, all of which need regular follow up contacts.

There are a ton of CRM's out there. We use Zoho CRM Plus. https://www.zoho.com/crm/crmplus/pricing.html

It has a higher learning curve than other programs, such as Salesforce, but the basic version comes with all sorts of extra features, so you save money in the long run. This will seem like an overkill at first, but after a few months you'll wonder how you ever lived without these tools.

In any case, try out the free trial versions of different CRM's to see what works best for you.

Communications

Many CRMs come with a voice-over-the-internet phone service and integrated email inbox. If yours doesn't for some reason, I'd strongly recommend purchasing a separate service and integrating it into your software. Feel free to forward incoming calls from the VOIP to your cell, but it's crucial that all your communications go through one central place. You want to be able to see at a quick glance every call, text and email sent to or received from a lead. Otherwise it's only a matter of time before you miss some critical request that will scuttle a lucrative deal that was nearly in the bag.

Workflow: Putting It All Together

In an ideal world, you or your assistants will be able to call and chat with every single lead the same day you learn about them. In practice though, things aren't going to go so smoothly. Your skip tracing service won't be able to find every phone number. In fact, even the most expensive services average around 75% accuracy. Then when you call, you're going to get a busy signal or voicemail quite often. And most of those you do reach won't give you an immediate "yes," "no" or "Here's my email. Send me more information" answer. They're too busy at the moment and want to reschedule. Usually after normal working hours or on the weekends.

Even if you're just contacting a small number of heavily vetted leads every month, keeping track of all this communication is going to drive you crazy and make you miss out on opportunities if you don't have a well-organized and comprehensive workflow written down. There are countless ways to customize this to suite your own needs, but every single trigger event and action step in "backend sales system" should be documented before you start contacting sellers.

The best way to do this is to create a training package as if you were onboarding a new employee with no real estate sales experience. Even if you don't plan on hiring an assistant now (you will one day as you scale up), writing everything out step by step is going to show you any weaknesses and blind spots in your system.

The exact details are going to vary depending on what software you're using and your own personal preferences. This can be as simple or as complicated as you like, but in broad strokes, you'll set up a workflow "pipeline" that moves through various stages or modules.

Take your snail mail campaigns to the next level

Yes, we're only targeting the hottest leads, but we're still facing all the traditional hurdles with mass mailings as everyone else. So we need to do things a little differently here.

To get the best open and engagement rates on your campaigns, while still keeping everything automated and easy to scale, you need to make sure your mailings are well organized and, above all, **personalized for each lead**. We didn't go through the trouble of filtering out the best leads just to send them some generic form letter.

1) Choose a provider. There are many mail automation services, but you must have one that offers mail merge options in the text, so you can send those custom offers to each lead. Click2mail is what we use. There are cheaper services, but they usually either don't offer mail merge or only send mailings every two weeks.

2) Create as many custom fields in your mailing list templates as possible. You need more customization than just the prospect's name in the greeting and the property address you want to purchase. The more custom fields you can insert, the better your letter will connect with the seller. At a minimum, you should customize:

- Your initial purchase offer. This doesn't have to be your max acquisition price, but it should be close if the property is in a high-demand neighborhood. Don't waste time with a generic low-ball offer. Whatever you do, don't just say "I want to purchase your property at…" You must include some specific dollar amount if you want the seller to respond.

- At least two specific details about the case. Such as the case # and name of the creditor in a foreclosure, the deceased's and attorney's name in probate, the tenant's name and amount of outstanding rent in evictions, etc… Your familiarity with their situation can generate instant rapport. At the very least, it'll make them curious how you knew so much.

- Replace any vague terms, such as "this area/neighborhood" or "this situation" with the field in your spreadsheet denoting the subdivision or case type for this lead. I know this sounds small, but there's a big difference between: "I was driving through your neighborhood..." and "I was driving through Spring Hills..."

3) Segment your master lead list by who gets a mailing.

Some leads, such as distressed multi-property owners or high equity properties in really hot neighborhoods are worth a full court outreach effort. Calling, snail mail, email, even knocking on the door.

But no one has the money and time to pour that much effort into every lead. There's an opportunity cost to everything, so you need some quick triggers to decide which leads get the royal treatment and which just get a letter/postcard.

There are many ways to set up your screening, and your rules will change as buyers come to you with specific requests. The simplest way to start is by looking at just the difference between amount owed and market value (I mean Zestimate, since we haven't gotten to the CMA phase yet).

Any property with less than 50% equity gets a letter. Odds are that'll cover the vast majority of your list. Those with more than 50% equity are added to the skip-tracing list and then the "to-call" module of your CRM.

4) Choose your delivery format.

There's a lot of debate about what type of mailing and packaging works the best, because every market is a little bit different. Personally, I use only two types of mailings:

Flat envelope with single letter. The open and conversion rate is great with these, since they really stand out and look important. But they are much more expensive. Save it for the niches where the owner is under less immediate pressure to sell, but have the potential to sell incredibly cheaply or are otherwise high value. Like probate, evictions and divorces.

5x8" Postcards. This is what we send to distressed homeowners, especially early foreclosures. The conversion rate is lower than a letter, but in net it's higher because the open rate is 100%. The trick is to still use mail merge to customize the postcard just like a letter and also add a link to your website to get free foreclosure defense information.

I generally recommend avoiding the standard folded letter. Yes, it's cheaper than the other options and so theoretically lets you target a wider audience for the same budget, but in practice the conversion rate is well below any other type of letter.

As for whether the letter should be handwritten (either for real or via machine) or typewritten is up to you. I have a personal bias against the handwritten letters. They seem so unprofessional. And in my one split-test of sending the same letter campaign with one version typed and one hand-written, the typed version got double the response rate.

However, I have many clients that swear by the handwritten approach. Maybe the secret is all about the calligraphy style. I don't know, so feel free to experiment and see what works best for you.

5) Test and evaluate different content.

There is no perfect, universal messaging script that works everywhere and at all times. So you have to constantly test different versions of your content.

To keep track of the response rates, it's a good idea to use a different call back number and website landing page for each version. And of course, make sure you also include a QR code to make it easier to visit your website.

Follow up schedule and content

Let me reiterate: The vast majority of the time you will not receive a firm yes or no answer when you first call someone or get the first call back from a letter.

This sales process requires building a relationship, or at a minimum a little bit of trust. So you'll need multiple contacts with the seller to seal the deal. But this doesn't have to be complicated or take a long time.

After that first phone call, you should either have the owner's email address or scheduled a face to face meeting, or both. If you weren't able to arrange either one, then you need a follow up texting (or call if they only have a landline) schedule.

I generally recommend one follow up the next day, another 3 days later and then after one week. If we're not getting engagement by then, meaning we haven't gotten the contract in their hands or they've stopped asking questions, I'll move them to the cold leads pile in the CRM and move on. Many of them will spring to live weeks later after no one else can beat your offer, but typically after one week you hit the point of diminishing returns if you keep contacting them on a regular basis.

Note: If you have the resources, it really helps to also monitor the upcoming foreclosure auctions and see if any of your cold leads have lost their appeals and now have an auction scheduled for this month. They'll be inundated with offers at this point, but since you've built up a little trust and rapport, they're usually willing to talk when you call, "Sorry to see they scheduled an auction. Have you filed a motion to…"

Most important with these contacts, you need to give them new, value-adding information each time you talk. Don't just call to "see how you're doing." Call to say, "You know, I found some information that could help in your situation…"

Of course, this is easy if the prospect is asking questions, but usually if they aren't converted after the first follow up, then they're stuck in the indecisive phase. We don't want them to forget about us or start shopping around for more offers, so we can achieve both objectives by sending them information that can help with their specific problem. If nothing else, you're at least keeping the conversation going.

For example, if they're in foreclosure, keep feeding them tips to delay the foreclosure. Anyway to fight the lender, such as consumer protection requests for documentation. There are a million tricks, so that's a topic for another book, but by now you should be working with your own attorney that can help you out.

The same goes for probate cases. There's even more legal minutia involved. The goal in both scenarios is to get the seller to view you as a competent ally in the process, and not just some random stranger that wants to buy their house and doesn't care about anything else.

Stages of the pipeline

Each niche is going to have a slightly different timeline, but they will all share the same general workflow (pipeline or lead status) in your CRM:

- Needs Contact – Segmented by high priority for calling and low priority for mailing.

- Needs Follow Up – Non-committal leads. You have no firm interest, but they're open to receiving more information. This is where the follow up schedule from the previous section comes in handy.

- Needs Attention – You have some interest, but the sellers need a hard sales approach to commit. You likely sent them or their attorney the unsigned contract, but no response yet. In larger organizations, this is where some 2nd level salesperson, like an acquisition's manager, would take over and visit the seller face to face.

- Ready for Action – Verbal commitment to sale. Here's where you need to run through your final due diligence fast and get your attorney to make any needed adjustments to the contract.

- Under Contract – Now the countdown to find a buyer begins. In a larger organization, this account would move to the investor outreach team. Send the property prospectus to every investor on your pre-vetted list

- Buyer Needs Attention – Buyers are interested, but want to negotiate or need some other assurance. Share all your data with them, the good, the bad and the ugly. The fewer unknowns they have, the faster they can execute.

- No Buyer – These are those rare contracts where none of your vetted buyers are willing to commit fast, even if you lower your assignment fee. Don't sit on the contract and try shopping it around to non-vetted buyers. Just activate your escape clause and inform the buyer ASAP. Clear your pipeline and free up resources for other deals, while letting the seller accept a backup offer with the minimum inconvenience for them.

- Buyer Assigned – Here's where you have the assignment agreement with the seller signed and their deposit in escrow. Only then do we send all the paperwork to the closing agent.

- Sent to Closing – These are the ready to execute contracts that have a closing date scheduled.

- Pending Contingency – These are assigned and ready to finish contracts, but no closing is scheduled yet because we're still waiting on something from the seller. For example, court approval in a probate sale.

- Closed – Payday!

Remember to keep the seller in the loop and notify them about each significant action. Even if it's bad news about a delay. Now that the offer has been accepted, you two are partners working to close the deal as fast as smoothly as possible. You need to keep their enthusiasm up.

This is especially crucial if your contract is "subject to…" anything. Such as the sale being approved by the court in an estate/probate sell. After doing all this work, it would be a shame for the seller to get cold feet just because they don't know what's going on.

Once a lead has moved to the Under Contract phase, schedule regular follow up phone calls at least once a week just to touch base with the seller. Even if you don't have anything to report. And of course, make sure your assistants know how to recognize when a signed seller is getting cold feet, so they can transfer the call straight to you.

Filtering And Prioritizing Leads.

Okay, so you have this spreadsheet full of the week's leads, and there were a lot more than you expected. Likely hundreds that need to be researched so you can customize your offer, plus skip tracing and calling them all.

In practice though, few organizations have the time nor resources to research the total property debt, CMA and Max Purchase Price on each lead. Or the marketing team and budget to contact everyone in a hurry. So to get the maximum return on your research and marketing expenses, you want to focus on the hottest wholesaling properties by screening out or sorting by:

- Remove any homeowner that's underwater. Short sales can be quite lucrative, I love them, but that's a totally different niche than wholesaling and needs its own book.

- Remove any homeowner that's within 30% of being underwater, based upon the Zestimate or whatever other automated tool you're using. In this initial screening, we only have the default or judgment amount for one particular financial event. The debt load is only going to climb once we search for other liens, so if we're starting so high, it's probably not worth your time to research these folks any further.

    These leads with some equity but not enough are also a huge time sink. If you send out mass mailings without screening for equity, the people on the verge of being underwater will call you back in large numbers out of sheer desperation, but they can't sell at a price that works for a wholesaler. You'll waste countless hours chatting with these homeowners, only to discover later that there's no way the numbers work out. Regardless of your assignment fee, it's just not mathematically possible for you to offer enough to satisfy the outstanding debt and clear title, while still presenting an attractive offer to end buyers.

- Downgrade any property that's too "old" for the neighborhood. As a wholesaler, you're attracted to the youngest properties around, since the older it is the likely more extensive the repair and renovation costs will be. So start with the newest inventory and work your way down the list.

A general rule of thumb is any property that's more than 30 years old is less interesting for wholesalers. Of course, this is a highly relative figure and a good example of how working with a local sales agent can add real value. In some markets, the average inventory age is much older. And in really fast-growing markets, even a 10-year-old property is considered ancient.

- Downgrade any property that's out of the ordinary for an area. Unless you have a buyer specifically requesting a certain type of investment, it's best for wholesalers to focus on the "average" units in a neighborhood. These boring places are so abundant because they have the most universal appeal. For example, you don't want to purchase the largest or smallest property on the block, nor anything with a "quirky" or "charming" character.

Which is why apartment complexes and cookie-cutter subdivisions make the best wholesaling hunting grounds.

- Downgrade any property that has hard to find comps. Creating an accurate CMA with a tight price range (smaller than 5% spread) is critical to determine your max purchase price and selling your deal to the end buyer. If we want to close fast and with high assignment fees, the buyer needs to see the genuine value of your deal in seconds. And nothing proves your value proposition better than seeing the price that clearly similar nearby properties sold for.

So the fewer recent sales of quite similar homes in close proximity to the subject, the less accurate your CMA will be. Which means the less interest you should have in reaching out to the seller. If you can't find three high-quality comps (see next section) that have sold in the same neighborhood in the last year, within sixty seconds, then this lead might not be worth your trouble.

- Red flag by neighborhood or zip code. Those in the hottest areas (i.e. most comp listings close in less than 3 months) move to the top of your list. You can offer the seller more money because the buyer can pay more, so you're far more likely to close these deals.

Those in colder neighborhoods get downgraded to a lower priority.

Now that you've weeded out the hard to wholesale properties, you won't waste time and money on dead ends. Then you simply prioritize this vetted list by giving the most attention to the people that have the most equity in the property. Don't filter by lowest to highest judgment amounts or highest property values, since those numbers alone are meaningless to a wholesaler. Equity is what you're buying and selling.

Obviously, the more equity the homeowner has—the space between the seller's breakeven point and the ARV—then the more room there is for you to make a win-win-win deal for the seller, the end buyer and yourself.

For example, if someone is going through foreclosure and owes the bank 90% of their home's market value, then there's not much a wholesaler can do for them. There's just no way to create a win-win-win situation here.

On the other hand, someone that owes only 20% will demand a higher price, but there's more wiggle room to negotiate. Not to mention that for the high-equity owner, foreclosure is not just a bad credit event. It's something extremely costly that's going to destroy all that equity. They're the ones most inclined to see you as an angel investor.

Note: When I say remove leads, I simply mean remove them from your "to contact" list. But you can still find use for all this data. Any distressed seller who's not yet listed on the market is a valuable lead to someone, even if they don't fit the stringent criteria for your wholesaling business.

So send those low equity deals directly to cash investors you want to butter up. There are many ways they could profit from them, for example by taking title via a QCD and fighting the foreclosure on the homeowner's behalf. All while collecting rent in the meantime and/or leveraging their surplus rights to outbid anyone else at auction.

If you also explain in detail why you're not following up on these leads, but realize they could have value for a direct investor, you'll really impress clients and stand out from the pack.

And no matter what, you can always send these leads to local listing agents to build up your connections. Spread the wealth and help them score some easy listings, and many will be happy to give you some free advice whenever you need it, such as helping you out with a free CMA on a hard to comp property.

Finding The Property's Real Wholesale Value

Even if you're a seasoned real estate pro that knows exactly how to put together a killer CMA and dissect every aspect of a potential deal at a distance, please don't skip this section. I'm breaking with traditional wisdom to create a system custom-tailored for wholesalers and not MLS buyers. And you should absolutely be using automated valuation tools, such as CoreLogic or IMAAP, to find comps and estimate value, but before signing you need to understand how to double check the algorithm's math.

When you're wholesaling, your property values must always be more conservative than the end buyer's analysis. Remember, you're not working on commission, but rather a flat rate per successful deal. So your number 1 concern is to make sure a deal goes down no matter what, with price a secondary concern.

One of the best ways to make sure a buyer will bite, regardless of the discount on the property or other contract details, is to make sure both of your ARV estimates match up. Let's be honest: The main reason wholesalers get a bad rap is that they're ARV estimates aren't reproducible. More often than not, the wholesaler's guess of what the property is worth after repairs is pure science fiction. And if they can't get this core data point right, how can a buyer trust anything else the wholesaler is saying?

When the buyer does their own CMA and estimates ARV, you want your client to be pleasantly surprised. They should value the property the same or maybe even higher than you did, but never for less. Otherwise, they won't trust anything else you have to say about the deal.

And not just this deal, since you're thinking bigger than that. You want to build a long-term partnership with the most deep-pocketed investors. No business ever went wrong by under promising and overdelivering.

So here's how wholesalers should evaluate the three key property values in real estate:

Comparative Market Analysis (CMA): Note - this is different for wholesalers than regular investors.

This is the first step to estimating how much a property is worth and how much you can offer the seller, but a CMA doesn't have to be complicated to be accurate. It's just simple math: the fewer variables in your model, the fewer potential errors and biases you can introduce. Remember, this is simply your comp report that considers *only* supply and demand in the target marketplace, and not the physical condition of the property itself. That's what current and after repair market values are for.

This means your CMA will always be a range of values covering the best case through the worst-case scenarios, rather than a specific dollar amount. If you have a lot of recent and quite comparable sales data available, then this range can be pretty tight, but there will always be some uncertainty.

I'm not trying to bore you with remedial real estate principles, but I'm trying to drive home the point that as wholesalers, we need to find a way to reduce the subjective nature of our CMA to gain the end buyer's trust and confidence.

There are a million little things you can factor when evaluating a property to arrive at the price you want. And the end buyer can do the same to drive down the price. Especially since you'll be dealing with only experienced investors who are on the lookout for cherry-picked comps that artificially inflate the subject's value. So the real trick is to choose comparable properties that are an easy "sell" to the buyer.

Because regardless of the details, if you can both agree on what is and what's not a legitimate comparable property, then everything else is just adjusting the margins. Fine-tuning the deal, but at least there will be a deal as long as you both agree on which comps to play with.

For example, you can go around in circles subtracting $X for having one less bedroom and adding $Y for more square footage, then wind up with a "comp" that doesn't have any physical resemblance to the subject property. Totally different style, lot size, amenities, different count of bedrooms, baths, square footage, etc ad nauseum.

Maybe that's all accurate and you have a long actuary sheet crediting and debiting every little change that would make your accountant proud... but you're not filing a tax return. You're trying to close a deal here. It's going to be a tough sell if the buyer has to double check a ton of math or just ignores your comps completely. Again, one of the crucial keys to scaling this business and wholesaling in bulk is to keep every deal as simple and transparent as possible.

So to keep things simple and easy to fact-check, we'll choose our comps solely by how many data variances there are from the subject, and by how much each variance can swing the value in any direction.

In practice, this simply means each comp should vary from the subject property by only one "Core" data point or (not and) two "Secondary" data points. You still have to estimate the value of these significant differences and explain them in your comp report, but the most important goal is to find high quality comparable properties in the first place. Again, you might make a different value judgment than the buyer for how much a particular feature adds or subtracts from the value, but as long as you both agree that this is a fair comp, then you shouldn't have any serious problems.

So at a minimum, you should include the following data with each comp, and make sure that only one of the core data points **or** not more than two of the secondary points are significantly different than the subject property.

Core data (Any variance from the subject, big or small, causes major value changes):

- Different subdivision/ neighborhood/ apartment complex
- Units
- Bedrooms
- Structure type
- Lot size

Secondary Data (Small variances are expected, but they need to be quite large to have a major impact on value):

- Baths (exact match)
- Square footage differences (if greater than +/-5%)
- Age difference (if greater than +/- 2 years)
- Construction style/façade
- Major features (pool, garage, patio, lake view, etc...)

Notes:

Of course, extreme variations in secondary data values can move that feature into the core data category. For example, a property that's 20 years older/newer than the subject or with a 25% larger/smaller living area is obviously going to swing the price quite a bit. But if you're following the general filtering steps from the previous phase, this should rarely be a problem. You'll only be focusing on subdivisions, apartment blocks and other planned neighborhoods where all the properties were built around the same time with roughly similar designs.

Also, your CMA is never done until you send the property report to the buyer. If you looked at the comps before first contacting a seller, but it then takes a few weeks before the owner is ready to sign, always check the comps again before sending the contract.

Additional screening:

At the risk of sounding like a broken record: as a wholesaler, your comps need to be more restrictive than the average investor's analysis. So if any of the sales you're looking at are older than one year or are not in the same subdivision/neighborhood or in an immediately adjacent subdivision/neighborhood, then they aren't reliable comps. A real estate agent might tell you otherwise, but we're not putting a property up for sale on the open market. We're wholesaling fast and off-market, so we need comps with impeccable credentials.

If you can't find three comps that match the admittedly strict criteria above, then it's probably not worth your time to continue pursuing this lead. Don't try to get creative or cast a wider geographic net. Just move on to a higher quality lead.

If you do decide to continue, realize that you must base your max purchase offer to the seller off the lowest band of your CMA range, since your comps are less than reliable.

More often though, once you've weeded out comps by number and severity of variances, you'll probably be left with more than three to choose from. It doesn't hurt to include these additional comps in your supplemental property report, but in the summary, you want just the three highest quality comps. Any less seems like you didn't do your homework and any more looks like you're playing math games to inflate the value. So you can prioritize which comps to consider in this order:

1. Distance from subject, obviously the closer the better.
2. Recent sales date. Newer the better. A more recent sale can take precedence over a closer sale if there is a large difference in time. For example, if you have two similar comps, but one occurred last month and the other ten months ago.
3. Value of the differences. Whichever variances change the value of the property by the least amount (either up or down) is the more reliable comp. For example, maybe comp 1 has adjustments that increase value by $10k, and comp 2 has adjustments that decrease value by $5k. Choose Comp 2, no matter how much it hurts. Again, it's not the difference between price and ARV that impresses experienced buyers. Only the accuracy and reliability of your prospectus will impress them.
4. If you're still undecided, then filter by which comps spent the least amount of time on market before being sold.

Note: This final screening on your CMA is also quite useful to help prioritize your marketing outreach, so never skip it. For example, if you notice that most of the comps in a particular neighborhood spent less than three months on market and sold at or above the listing price, then clearly this area is in high demand. So prioritize leads in this neighborhood and make sure you roll out the red carpet when you contact these sellers.

On the other hand, if most of the comps are taking longer than six months to sell and/or need large price reductions to close, then you're looking at a colder market that should be lower on your priority list.

Example Comp Evaluation:

Subject property:

Type: Single Family Home, Ranch-style, concrete block w/stucco exterior
Units/bed/baths: 1/3/2.5
Lot/heated living area: 1 acre/1,600 sq ft
Built: 2007
Features: 2 car attached garage, 400 sq foot attached porch

We have four sales in the subdivision that are less than one year old.

1. Comp 1 is on a 0.75 acre lot, but all other core and secondary features match. This is a **good comp**, since it's easy to adjust for a single variable. It's not a great comp though, because the variance is on a core feature that can radically change value.

2. Comp 2 matches all the core features, but has only 2 baths, sq footage that's 10% bigger and has a pool. This is a **bad comp**, since you have three different points to adjust for. Together they could add up to a significant value change. The whole thing does not intuitively look like a comp for the end buyer.

3. Comp 3 matches all the core features, but has a different style and is five years older. This is an **ok comp**, since even though you're adjusting for two numbers, they're smaller features that won't drastically change the total value.

4. Comp 4 is similar to #3, with only two secondary variances. Say a 1-car garage and 10% smaller sq footage. However, upon further screening, you realize that it is across the street from the subject

house, whereas #3 is a block away. Or maybe #4's sale was closed last month and #3 closed six months ago. Either way, this is the **best comp** so far because the proximity and/or freshness of the sale makes it the most relevant comp, regardless of the change in value.

So in this idealized example, you now have three comps that are easy for a buyer to agree with, without having to dive into every +/- value adjustment modifier.

Current Market Value (CMV):

Many wholesalers don't bother including this value, since they're looking to present the property in the best light possible. To be fair, it's not strictly necessary, but adding the current as-is market value below the much higher ARV makes your offer more credible for end buyers. This value is something that experienced flippers will work out on their own to determine their risk exposure on every deal. So if they see that you did the homework yourself, even if they disagree with your result, they'll still be impressed that you understand their concerns. You'll definitely build trust and stand out from any other wholesaler.

And it doesn't take but a few seconds, since you're already gathering all the information you need from the CMA and ARV.

CMV is simply the price you can realistically expect to sell the property for on the open market in the near term (less than six months), in current market conditions, in "as is" condition. Or in the eyes of your end buyer, the minimum value of this investment right now, without investing a single cent.

This is fairly easy to gauge. Start with the mid-point of your CMA range, then discount for every broken/worn out item or anything that hurts curb appeal. This is pure subtraction, without any positive additions. It's quite possible that your current market value will be lower than your minimum CMA band, but it can't be higher than the mid-point of your CMA range.

After Repair Value (ARV):

This is a more optimistic figure that assumes you'll unlock every penny of the property's value, if you're willing to invest in repairs. I'm going to break from traditional wisdom here, because we're focusing on ARV from a wholesaler's perspective. Which means you should calculate it a little differently before presenting this value to a potential buyer.

Now, you'll still need to figure out a ballpark estimate of the cost of all repairs to get the property up to living standards (fixing broken doors, faucets, patching drywall, replacing worn carpeting, etc...) and staging costs (landscaping, painting, assorted cosmetics...) to maximize market value. But that's just so you can figure out how high you can push your assignment fee.

In practice, don't expect the buyer to put much stock in your cost estimates. You're not footing the bill for repairs, so they're going to get their own GC to go through the property. And quotes among contractors are all over the place, regardless of the property condition. So that means unless the buyer is also hiring you to do the repairs, your estimates are just interesting trivia for them and not part of their decision-making process. If some buyer you haven't been working with on many deals does rely on your estimates... well, that's a red flag that they're quite inexperienced and new to the game.

In any case, every buyer will pay attention to your ARV, regardless of how much you say it'll cost to reach that level. If your value estimate comes in higher than theirs, you can bet they'll be skeptical of everything else you have to say.

So to avoid this, just like when estimating the current market value, we'll stick to our CMA bands. That means your maximum ARV is simply the high-end, "best case scenario" of your CMA range, with repairs estimated separately. No other variables to consider. This way if the buyer challenges your ARV, you don't have to spend time justifying some subjective analysis. You can simply point to your easy to read comps and let the math speak for itself.

Note: ARV has nothing to do with value adding renovations or expected market trends. It's just the top value from your CMA range, without any other factors involved. An easy number to fact check. If there's some other factor that you're convinced is going to drive up the value in a few months, then include that in your general notes on the property. Not here.

For example, say you look at comps on a property and come up with a CMA ranging from $200-$220k before you ever see the property. After getting inside, you realize the property is in excellent shape. Just about turnkey ready. Nonetheless, you peg your Current Market Value at the mid-point of $210k. Odds are it could fetch more right now, but you're being pessimistic in the CMV.

In the ARV field, you can list $220k, with <$1,000 in estimated repair costs. If it turns out you were wrong and the contractor's quote came out to $5,000, it's not a deal breaker. The buyer might be annoyed, but they can't fault you because your value estimate hasn't changed. At this point, their trust in you isn't seriously shaken.

Screening Leads To Determine Your Max And Initial Offer

When we first start out with coaching, many wholesalers I'm mentoring think I'm way overcomplicating things at this point. They'll usually say something like: "Why bother with all of this number crunching and estimating? Can't I just set a hard limit of never paying more than 50% of the property's Zestimate? No matter what's wrong with the place, I'm guaranteed to sell the contract to someone really fast at some level of profit."

And that's true in theory, but in the real world, how much inventory are you going to get under contract with low-ball offers like that? Outside of a free-falling housing market, like back in 08-09, how many sellers do you think are going to give you the time of day? The only ones that might be tempted are not just distressed, but truly desperate...and you can bet you're not the only cash buyer trying to woo them.

In practice, there will always be someone with more money and a higher risk tolerance than you. **So never give them the chance to outbid you.** You can't beat their max price, but you can top their initial offer. When you first contact a seller, skip the games and give them a good to great quote right off the bat. Either your max purchase price if the property is in a hot neighborhood or a bit less for average areas. Even if the seller turns you down immediately, every cash buyer that calls after you will be at a disadvantage.

If these other buyers even give a quote when they first call, they'll always start with an extremely low-ball purchase offer, usually around 40-50% of ARV. Maybe they'll attempt to "wow" the seller by agreeing to go as high as 60%, after an hour or so of negotiation. In some cases, perhaps even 70% if they can inspect the property and it's in amazing condition. But if you already quoted the seller 60% in the first few seconds of your outreach, you've set the floor even if the seller wasn't interested at the moment. They won't even bother entertaining these crappier offers that come later and will usually hang up before your competitors have a chance to increase their price. You've rigged the game and stacked the deck in your favor.

Then when you follow up with the seller a week later on the phone, you can bet they're going to be happy to talk again.

And when they ask, "Is your offer still on the table?" Then guess who has the negotiation leverage.

Of course, to make all this happen you need a way to estimate your max offer with confidence, and with precision over many deals. The only way to do this is by evaluating the deal through the eyes of your end buyer.

You already have the property value from the last step. So we just need to know the buyer's goal (We'll gather this information in phase 4). Then you can estimate the buyer's total costs and compare that to the seller's minimum price (sum of all their liens). The larger the spread between the two, the better the chance you have to make a deal.

The classic criteria for finding your maximum allowable offer is to just subtract 30% from the ARV-your assignment fee. And while that's a perfectly safe strategy to make sure you don't overpay, it doesn't tell you what your initial offer should be. If you're just guessing about your initial offer or, even worse, waiting until the seller name's a price, you'll run into two major issues:

1) You'll waste countless hours on the phone with homeowners that can't sell at the discount you need, simply because they're underwater or nearly so on their mortgage and other liens. This is all avoidable because you could find this information within minutes from the courthouse records and never even bother contacting these people.

2) Even worse, you're going to blow the opportunity to close so many deals and scale things up because you're trying to maximize per-deal profit rather than maximize inventory under contract.

You only need such a huge equity cushion if you don't know anything about the property or you're dealing with inexperienced, skittish buyers.

Neither one applies to your situation, since we're working with only the most experienced buyers and we can find the seller's breakeven price from the court records. Since we can remove so many unknowns, we can close deals with less than 30% equity involved. Which opens the door to a whole new class of wholesale deals. You're no longer limited to buying just from the most desperate sellers with dilapidated, vacant properties. You can now buy properties that are in near market-ready states, but that most wholesalers would ignore because the price is too high for their arbitrary risk level.

The best properties, i.e. those with the lowest rehab costs and in the most desirable neighborhoods, are always going to fetch higher prices, even if you're working off-market. For example, what if you found a property that's going through foreclosure. The owners have already given up on the place and have been doing short-term Airbnb rentals. So the asset is in near turnkey ready condition. And when you look at the comps, you see that every similar place in the neighborhood sold at the listing price and within two months.

From the end buyer's perspective, whether they plan to flip or rent it, this is a low-risk investment. There aren't any major unknowns about how high the ARV will be and how much it'll cost to unlock that price.

So you hop on the phone and immediately offer the seller 70% of the ARV... only to hear them sigh and give you a muttered "I'll keep you in mind." They didn't even bother to make a counteroffer.

But with a quick glance at the court records, you'd see that the seller's mortgage and other liens comes out to 75% of the ARV. You were so close. If you had started with that amount in your initial offer, then quite likely you could have come out with a deal that covers all the seller's debt and still leaves 15-20% equity for the end buyer after your fee.

Finding your max offer for a quick flip or if you don't know what the end buyer's goals are:

The formula for finding your initial and max offer is still the same as everyone else is using. ARV – a discount rate and your fee. However, we're doing some more research so we can estimate your initial offer with confidence *before* contacting the seller.

1) This is a gamechanger, because so few wholesalers are able to do this right off the bat. They call, ask if the owner is interested in selling, then ask a bunch of questions while avoiding giving a price. Then they crunch the numbers and call back with an initial, extremely low ball offer. They're willing to negotiate higher, but can you imagine how frustrating it is for the seller to spend so much time on the phone, only to get hit with an arbitrarily low purchase offer?

They will love that you've already done your homework and can offer then a price immediately that's higher than everyone else's (while still below your max price).

2) With this approach, you don't have to guess at your assignment fee. You can look at the deal and see exactly how much you can mark it up, while keeping the buyer and seller happy. Usually you'll find that setting an arbitrary fee of $5k or $10k is a mistake because you're leaving too much money on the table. Other times, you'll realize that even with a sub $5k fee, there's not enough profit for the buyer and seller to get them both interested. So then you can move on to a higher quality lead before you've invested any time on the phone.

Step 1:

Find the subject property ARV from the high end of your comps = $250k

Note: If your CMA price range is large, then use the midpoint instead of the ARV to estimate costs.

Step 2:

Estimate the buyer's post acquisition costs. If you're brand new to real estate, then you're going to need a local agent to guide you through this process the first few times you do it. The cost of labor, insurance, landscaping, etc... varies so much in each market. But with a little practice, you'll be able to create your own estimates with confidence in a hurry.

The hardest part is going to be the repair costs, since you haven't seen the property yet. But at the moment, you can ballpark this with a generic number for your marketplace. For example, in the initial analysis before seeing the property, I'll budget $10k or 10% of ARV, whichever is higher, for rehab. Then adjust as needed once we've contacted the seller and completed the rest of our due diligence.

If there are any extensive, major repairs needed, you'll discover this in your pre-signing due diligence or during the inspection phase.

$34,500 = Buyer's post acquisition costs for a flip in less than 6 months.

- Repair costs to get full ARV: $10k
- Staging costs: $2k
- 6 months of carrying costs: $6k
  Assuming the average time on market in this neighborhood is 6 months)
- Closing costs on each end: $16,500k
  Assuming 2.5% ($4,000) buying at $160k and 5% ($12,500) of selling at $250k.

$25k = Margin of error (10% of ARV). In the absence of more information, we'll use this as a proxy for the buyer's minimum expected profit.

Add the flipping costs and expected profit (you can call this a margin of error) together and subtract from the ARV and you get:

$190,500 = Buyers maximum anticipated purchase price

Step 3:

Now we add up all those liens on the property. If in foreclosure, you'll have to guess a little to determine the payoff balance with all the back interest, court and attorney fees. That could increase the default amount significantly. Your title attorney can help you come up with a general calculator for this.

The end result is the seller's breakeven point, where if they sold for less they would lose money:

$150k = Seller's minimum price needed to pay off all debts

So we have a $40k spread between the seller's breakeven point and the buyer's max offer. Whatever difference there is between the two figures is your profit.

If you could get both parties to sell and buy at the limit of their tolerances, then you could make up to $40k in this deal. Realistically, you're going to have to dip into your potential profit in order to make the deal happen.

If you were happy to settle for a $10k fee, then you have $30k you can split up among both parties.

So set your initial offer price in the middle of this range, so $165k.

The highest you're willing to go will be $180k (Buyer's $190k max minus your $10k fee).

Phase III - Locking Down Contracts

Initial Outreach To Sellers

So with all this data at your fingertips, it's tempting to just mass mail a thousand flyers out or mass text a thousand leads. But remember, as a wholesaler you're a real estate professional, and real estate is all about making a human connection. It's *not* a numbers game. So that means picking up the phone and calling folks is still the best way to get maximum engagement.

I need to harp on this a little bit more because this is the step where I lose a lot of wholesalers. Many are doing this part-time at first and the idea of spending all their free hours on the phone is a deal breaker. And finding and training a qualified assistant to do the initial calling for you is a slow process. I get that.

So as a compromise, at least segment your lead list. For example, if you have 1000 leads this week, call the 10 or 100 highest value ones yourself, such as the most distressed homeowners with the newest properties in the most desirable neighborhoods. For all the rest, you can send them a letter or text message for the initial contact.

Contacting attorneys versus owner/rep directly

In some niches, such as probates or evictions, it's quite easy to get the attorney contact information for the home seller. Attorneys can be a useful secondary point of contact if you're having trouble reaching the homeowner, since the lawyer is obligated to pass along any offer to their client and people are far more likely to pay attention to their attorney than some random stranger. They can also make a useful partner in the probate niche, since these lawyers are often deferring some or all of their fees until the property is sold. So their interest is simply "clearing the books" as fast as possible, which is where a cash investor really shines.

With that said, remember that any attorney is just a steppingstone on the way to contacting the decision maker and can never replace talking directly to the homeowner or estate rep. I've seen too many wholesalers just send off emails or letters to attorneys in mass, without skip tracing the owner, and then wonder why their response rate is so low.

So if the contact has an attorney listed in the court documents, then it helps to send a formal letter of intent to the lawyer at the same time you call the owner. The letter of intent isn't a binding contract. The price and terms will change later, but this is a useful part of the multi-channel outreach effort.

Proof of funds request

Getting to the last phase of a potential deal and having the seller request some documentary proof that you have the money available to close this deal is one of the greatest worries for many new wholesalers, but this minor administrative detail should be the least of your concerns. Since you're dealing directly with homeowners or estate representatives, rather than brokers, the odds of them even asking you for proof of funds are quite slim. Especially if you're conducting yourself in a professional manner.

If anyone does ask and you don't have the capital handy, don't panic. Be transparent but confident with the seller. Confidence is one of the most contagious diseases known to man.

For example, you could simply say:

"I'm afraid I don't personally have the capital handy at the moment, but I have several investors who I've worked with in the past that are interested in partnering with me. I just need to choose which one can close this deal the fastest. We'll hammer the details on our end within 48 hours and can immediately begin the closing process. In fact, let's go ahead and schedule an appointment with the closing agent for this Saturday. What time works best for you?"

There are so many ways you can word your response, but keep it short (don't dwell on details), attentive (confident but not dismissive of the seller's concern) and relaxed (you're unfazed by this little hiccup). Then address the seller's real concern: speed of closing. If they're asking for proof of funds, what they're really asking for is assurance that you can close fast.

If for some reason the seller is still concerned and insists on seeing proof of funds before signing the contract, you can offer to increase your earnest money deposit or even shorten the closing window to two weeks instead of the usual month. Gently remind them that they are free to accept backup offers in the meantime.

And if somehow this isn't enough and they still refuse to sign the deal without proof of funds, then you're better off moving on to someone else. C'est la vie. Your time is better spent helping someone who's really motivated to sell fast. But this scenario is exceedingly rare, because it means you weren't dealing with a truly motivated seller in the first place. I only even mention it so that you're well informed and not blindsided if you run into a recalcitrant seller, but this rare problem is not something you need to worry about on a regular basis.

Primary goals on the first phone call

1. Provide your detailed offer right off the bat. Give only the most bare-bones introduction about who you are and then state your offer. This will qualify and stage the prospect immediately, without needing to ask if they're willing to sell and for how much. It also ensures that you sink your hook into them, even if they're unwilling to entertain your offer at the moment

2. Ask about the prospect's goals specifically, but in general try to spark a conversation about their situation. This creates rapport and trust instantly. Keep the conversation natural though and don't just run through a checklist of generic questions. Frame all your responses to what they say as open-ended questions, and not yes/no ones, to keep the chat flowing.

3. Get the seller's email to send them either a sample contract or more information about how we can help in their situation (I.E. tips to fight creditors/speed up probate).

   Note: We'll send them a ready to go contract, except that we haven't signed it yet. Once we have their verbal agreement, then we'll run through the due diligence steps at the end of this chapter before we sign.

4. If they want to negotiate price already, transfer directly to you if you're available. Otherwise, schedule a follow up call or in person visit. Same if they refuse to give their email.

5. If time permits, ask due diligence follow-up questions (from the list at the end of this chapter).

General Rules For Contacting Sellers:

✓ Your number 1 goal when first contacting a seller is to spark a conversation. Make your offer and then ask about their situation and goals. If you do that, then getting the property under contract will come eventually. Even if they flat out tell you they're uninterested in your offer, you should still send them more information about other options. Suggest various foreclosure defense services/tips that they might not know about. If nothing else, ask for an email to send them your comp report so they can see what the property is worth. If you can just get them to talk about their problems and walk them through their options to get out of trouble, then your offer will always be at the top of their mind.

✓ When calling, texting or leaving a voicemail, don't bother mentioning the word "cash" in the initial contact. You can point out that this is an all-cash offer when they propose a higher price, but you don't want to give a bad first impression. If the seller has been contacted by another wholesaler already, they're going to bristle when they hear the word "cash" and expect another insulting low-ball offer or amateurish sales tactics.

- ✓ Always, always and always proofread your communications for typos. Even if you're copy/pasting template data, make sure you got their name right and didn't add extra spaces. A single error will scream spam and guarantee that you're wasting your time. You absolutely want to come across as a trustworthy professional who knows what they're talking about.

- ✓ Avoid yes/no questions in your initial contact. Ask open-ended questions to get more engagement. This adds an obstacle in the way of their knee-jerk response to put off difficult decisions or say no to unsolicited offers, while making them pause to really consider what you're saying. For example, don't say "Is this property for sale?" Instead, ask "What are your plans for the property?" It sounds so small, but this simple tweak makes a world of difference.

- ✓ Always call the asset for sale the "property" or something neutral like that, instead of saying "home" or "house." It doesn't help anyone to remind the distressed seller of their emotional attachment to the place.

- ✓ **Include a dollar amount in your initial contact instead of a general statement about purchasing the property.** This can be a specific cash offer to purchase or just listing the total debt on their property that you can take off their hands. We'll negotiate that value up or down later during the follow up, but including a hard number in the first contact increases the call back rate exponentially.

    Hardly anyone ever does that, so you'll really stand out. Afterall, maybe your offer is low, but you're giving more information than any of the other cash investors contacting them, so calling you back has the fewest unknowns. Just by offering a hard number, you've already built up a small but noticeable level of rapport right off the bat.

- ✓ If you aren't confident in your CMA or investor analysis skills yet, then use a 3rd party automated service to estimate home value during your initial screening. Just take their comp price minus 35% for your initial cash offer (assuming it's higher than the default). For example, if the property's estimated value is $200k, we would offer $130k in cash during the initial contact. It might be scary making such an offer without looking at the comps yourself, but you can always adjust this later after you've found out more about the property and the homeowner's situation. You can also always hire a professional agent to get a solid CMA before sending the final contract.

- ✓ When calling, make no explicit or even implicit mention of "debt" or "foreclosure" or any other negative point until you are 100% positive you're speaking to the homeowner and doing so in private. This means even identifying yourself as a "foreclosure expert." These are sensitive subjects and the people you're contacting are not usually in the best mood. It doesn't matter how great your offer is if you insult them by airing their dirty laundry in front of others. For example, when you're skip tracing a phone number, you only know that the number is associated with the subject name and address. Depending upon the quality of your data, you could be calling a parent, sibling, cousin, even friend of the owner.

- ✓ Let them tell their story! I know, I get it. Time is valuable and after you've been doing this for a little while you'll grow jaded and sick of all the excuses and sob stories. But building rapport is basic salesmanship 101 stuff. After you've gotten the key details across, let the owner do the talking. Or as the saying goes, "Be 30% interesting and 70% interested."

The single biggest outreach mistake I see with most wholesalers is they ram the merits of their offer down the prospect's throat and hardly let them get a word in edge wise. Besides coming off as too aggressive and not building rapport, how can you find out what the homeowner's pain points are and how you can help? Or to appeal to the greediest among us, what if they don't have a clue how much equity is in the property and they just need enough cash to move out? By pushing your offer too hard, you're implying that the property is in high demand and/or you're desperate to make a deal. Either way, you're shooting yourself in the foot.

- ✓ Never lose sight of the big picture: the ultimate goal is not to get them to make a firm commitment over the phone. Rather, we want to A) make a connection and be seen as a partner. An angel investor. B) Get the contract paperwork or some other information in their hands via email. This puts us heads and shoulders above any other investor that comes along later, regardless of what price they're offering.

- ✓ Your follow up needs to add real value. Don't just call or text a few days later to see if they've changed their mind. Instead, leverage the information you've learned about their situation to keep the conversation going by asking pointed questions or giving useful advice. For example, you can share foreclosure defense tips, share your CMA, ask if they've done X, Y, Z...

Sample Scripts And Mailings

There are a million ways to word these, so this is just to get your creative juices flowing. Stick to what feels natural for you.

Most of these scripts are intended as training materials for a first level calling assistant to use, so adjust the greeting for whoever is using them.

Cold Contact Direct Mail Flyer (Foreclosure)

Dear <owner_first_name> <owner_last_name>,

My name is __ and I would like to make you a cash offer to purchase your property at <Owner_street_address> for <Initial_bid> as soon as possible.

Unfortunately, it appears as though <plaintiff_name> has begun foreclosure proceedings against your home. If they haven't served you notice yet, here is the case number <case_#> so you can read the details yourself. I understand how unfair and frustrating this situation must be, which is why I'm ready to help by purchasing your property 100% as-is with a cash payment. You'll be able to immediately pay off the mortgage loan and all other liens or taxes owed on the property.

If you have no interest in moving away and you're only being forced to abandon your home because of the foreclosure and impending eviction, we have several options to help you stay there debt-free or fight your lender. For example, did you know that 98% of all mortgages contain accounting errors or outright consumer protection law violations committed by the lender? We can put you in touch with experienced foreclosure defense attorneys that will help you find and document these errors, giving you significant leverage over the lender and even entitling you to a direct cash settlement in most cases.

In some cases, we can even purchase the property and lease it back to you at a reasonable rental rate. In all cases though, we will take over the property's debt, freeing you completely from the financial burden you currently face, as well as put immediate cash in your pocket in exchange for assuming the property's ownership.

Please note that I'm only able to work out a deal before the foreclosure process is complete. At that point, the lender will take control and put the home up for sale at auction. Since you have only a short window of time to work out a solution to this problem, it's important that you contact me by phone at ___ or email at ___ as soon as possible. Please feel free to send me any questions you have, big or small.

[Note: Be careful that you don't actually give specific legal advice if you're not an attorney.]

Cold Contact Direct Mail Flyer (Probate)

Dear «First_Name» «Last_Name»,

My name is __ and I'm a real estate investor that would like to purchase the property at «property address» as soon as possible.

After looking online, I'm sorry to see that the owner has passed away and you have petitioned the court for probate administration I've had to do that once for my family, so I understand how difficult this process can be.

Whenever you are ready, we can help by taking this property off your hands so you don't need to invest in any repairs, cleaning, landscaping or anything else. We can lock in the contract now, file it with the court and it will be executed once the court releases the property to sell. No need to spend so much money and time preparing the house to sell and waiting for a buyer's mortgage lender to approve financing. We can have the entire purchase amount wired to your account within hours of executing the contract, and hopefully provide everyone in your family some stress relief. I'm familiar with your probate attorney, so if you're interested, I'm happy to forward the paperwork to their office for them to review everything first.

If you have other plans for the property, please let me know and I'll see what I can do. My investor network is quite large and flexible, which affords us many options to help your family in any situation. Please don't hesitate to ask me any questions, big or small. I aim to make this whole process as stress-free as possible.

Thank you for your time and God bless you and your family.

For SMS and Voicemail

Here you need to get your message across even faster than when talking directly to a prospect, but at least there won't be any interruptions. These messages will get across all the key information the prospect needs to know and how to take action without requiring any additional steps. All while doing so in a more personal, professional way than most cash buyers.

Message to subject:

Hello, I'm trying to reach <contact name>. My name is <agent name>. My partner and I would like to purchase your property at <address> for <max bid> today. Whenever you have a moment, please give me a call back or email me at <your email>. Thank you and have a great day.

Message to other relative if you don't receive a call back:

Hello, I'm trying to reach <contact full name>. My name is <agent name> and I'm a real estate investor who would like to purchase your property at <address> for <max bid> today. Whenever you have a moment, please ask <contact first name> to give me a call back or email me at <your email>. Thank you and have a great day.

First contact by voice (pre-foreclosure)

*(Good morning/afternoon/evening), my name is __ and I'm trying to reach __ about making a purchase offer for __ on the property in (*name of city*).*

From here, it's really important to focus on what their goals are and getting an email to send them more information about how you can help. They aren't in foreclosure yet, so they actually have the option of doing a regular sale. Since they're under a little less pressure, they'll be slower to commit.

First contact by voice (probate)

*(Good morning/afternoon/evening), my name is __ and I'm trying to reach __ about making a purchase offer on the property in (*name of city*).*

[Try to speak this whole line without interruption or long pauses. Stay calm and don't rush your speech though. Pause when you're done to give them a moment to respond.]

I'm a real estate investor who has purchased many properties in this neighborhood. My partner and I are prepared to offer you $ __ in cash to purchase the property in as-is condition.

[Short pause]

I know from personal experience how frustrating this probate process can be, so at least we can offer you a signed purchase contract ready to be executed as soon as the court appoints you the administrator. No need for you to invest a single penny in repairs or maintenance, nor wait months to get the property ready for sale.

[Pause for response.]

I'd love to schedule a time to come by and show you our offer…

[If at any point they're too busy to discuss things further, simply say:]

I understand completely. You know, I'm familiar with your probate attorney. I'll just forward them the details for you to go over when you have time. Does that work?

Of course, after the first line you're playing it all by ear. Adapt to their emotional state and really listen to what they're telling you.

Remember: The ultimate goal is not to get them to make a firm commitment over the phone. Rather, we want to learn their goals and get the contract paperwork in their hands to peruse. This puts us heads and shoulders above any other investor that comes along.

If they're receptive and want to talk more, then we want to learn more about their situation while building rapport. Some additional questions you'll want to ask with probate properties:

- Don't ask this directly, but listen for signs that some other family member is a key influencer. For example, the probate petitioner is the son of the deceased, but he keeps mentioning concerns from his wife, sister, etc... Offer to contact that other influencer and take the stress of him by talking to them directly.
- Do they have any questions about the probate or selling process?
- Are there any other extraneous factors? For example, someone is squatting in the house, they're worried about having cash for attorney fees, another family member doesn't want to sell, etc...

Adapting on the fly to common interruptions

In the real world, there will be all sorts of interruptions that keep you from sticking to your script. However, if the seller is still on the line after interjecting, that means they're still giving you a chance to sway them, no matter what they said. Now, this politeness won't last long, so you need a well-thought out reflexive response handy. You'll have just seconds to salvage the situation and get the conversation back on track, so no time to hem and haw and think of a reply.

1) A snort, laugh, exasperated sigh, muttering under the breath, etc...

[Note: Don't let anything faze you. Stay confident, upbeat and keep talking like nothing happened.]

We would purchase the property in its current condition. Which means we could close in just a matter of days and you don't have to spend a penny on maintenance, repairs, staging the property or any of that other rigmarole.

2) Wrong number or right number but wrong person.

Oh, I'm sorry. They gave me the wrong number here. How can I reach Mr./Ms. __ about buying their property at __ for $X in cash?

[Note: You might get a bad number from your skip tracing service, but odds are this person is a family member or acquaintance of the one you're trying to contact. So we still want to get the cash offer in their hands to boost engagement, whether they give us the right number or not.]

3) I'm busy right now.

No problem. I'm happy to email you my offer so you can read it over at your leisure and then schedule a call for a better time. What email address should I send it to?

[Note: No matter what they say, we have their number so we can call back another time. Right now we want to add to our knowledge and get their email.]

4) Not interested in selling at any price.

Oh, no problem. If you could tell me a little more about your long-term plans, I'm sure we can help you achieve them. For example, if you're planning on renting the place out, we've partnered with one of the largest property management companies in the area. One that doesn't charge management fees if the property is unoccupied.

5) Can't sell. I haven't been appointed administrator yet.

No worries. That's not a problem for us. We can lock in the contract and just include a "contingent on seller being awarded probate administration." Then you have a guaranteed cash buyer ready to execute the contract the moment probate is finished. Should only take a few days to distribute the funds to everyone.

Pause.

In fact, I understand how expensive this process is. So we can even cover your attorney fees to make sure this process goes as fast as possible.

5) Our price is way too low. They want a deal-breaking price that's at, near or even above market value.

Well, I have many partners, each with different investing budgets. So I'm sure we can work something out. Since seeing is believing, the first thing I want to do is send you my comparative market analysis for your property. Then you can see exactly how much your property is worth and how investors come to that conclusion. What is your email address?

6) Can't sell because the bank has already foreclosed.

[Note: You might be surprised by how many homeowners think that Lis pendens or trustee sale notice signals the end of foreclosure, rather than just the beginning.]

Oh, that's the good news. This early in the foreclosure process, there are many things we can do to fight the bank. And you absolutely have the right to pay off your creditor at any time before the auction is held and stop the foreclosure. This is where we can really help, because we can close in just five business days and end this nightmare fast, before the lender starts inflating the amount owed with ridiculous attorney fees, back interest and all their other tricks...

7) But the bank said I can't sell because the foreclosure process isn't complete...

As I'm writing this book in an ultra-hot real estate market in most areas of the country, we're coming across more and more homeowners that were told by their lender that they can't legally sell a property that's in foreclosure. This is, of course, utter nonsense. Under the universally accepted "right of redemption," the debtor has the right to satisfy a lien holder at any time up until the day the auction takes place. In many states, even for a certain number of days after the auction.

Sometimes this misunderstanding comes about because of an honest miscommunication between the homeowner and lender, but more often than not you're looking at a shady lender/loan servicer that's straight up lying to the homeowner.

And if the forecloser is lying to the homeowner, that's a red flag that there's some serious equity in the property. The creditor must believe they stand to profit more from an auction or later REO sale than by being paid off right now. So you should jump on these opportunities.

Ask the seller to demand a payoff letter from the bank, which includes attorney fees, court filing fees, back interest and everything needed to satisfy the mortgage.

Under Federal law, the lender has to send this within 7 business days, or a "reasonable amount of time" if in foreclosure (12 C.F.R. § 1026.36.). Have the seller stress that if they don't return it soon, they'll file a notice of error (12 C.F.R. § 1026.35.).

Distressed Homeowner Common Objections and Solutions

Owner understands how much equity they have in the home and refuses to sell at a steep discount.

Solution: Find out their end game. Are they hoping on negotiating some settlement with the bank or a traditional home sale? Gently point out how that ship has already sailed. Stress how their equity is evaporating fast with all the extra interest and attorney fees, plus they'll need extra cash to get the home ready for sale, all while they're racing against the foreclosure clock. Add in agent fees and no time to hold out for a good offer and they'll be lucky to have any equity left over.

And don't just talk in the abstract. Show them the numbers you ran on their home. Share your information on the estimated final judgment debt and realistic fast property sale price (not just ARV). In most cases, a quick cash sell to you would truly leave them with far more money in their pockets, without all the risk or stress. The fastest way to convince them is to show them your data.

Worst case scenario, you wind up losing all your bargaining room and pay top-dollar for the property. Doesn't matter, since you still built in enough equity in the deal to ensure you and end buyers can profit, or else you wouldn't have called them. The key thing is you're still converting this hot lead and closing the deal fast, before anyone else. Smaller profit, but safe and rapid deals are a great way to build a sustainable real estate empire.

Owner flat out says they have no interest in moving, no matter what price you offer.

Seller refuses to leave for sentimental or other life reasons and plans on "getting a lawyer to fight those SOB's."

Solution: No problem. This might seem like a deal breaker at first, because all they're doing is delaying the inevitable foreclosure and chewing up equity in the meantime. And no, it's not the ideal flipping opportunity, but there's still some serious money to be made for all parties in this situation. Remember, even if we can't directly profit from the deal, we can pass it along to someone else who can as a perk of doing business with us. For example, this is the type of scenario where a direct cash investor can swoop in and purchase the property with a quit claim deed and lease the home back to the seller. Plus, once they actually talk to lawyers and see how much it's going to cost and how low their chances of success are, they'll come around to the idea of a quick sale eventually.

So instead of trying to change the seller's mind, I'll point out how that's a great idea. Where other investors are backing out at this point or mentioning all the flaws with their plan, I'm going to work with the owner and help them make their dream come true. I'll offer some tips on the foreclosure delay approach and explain how, if they get a good attorney that's really working in their interest, they could delay the foreclosure for years.

Even better, after we've established a little rapport and they have a general understanding of everything that's involved, I'll offer a lease-back option. I'll assume title and fight the bank on their behalf. I'll pay all the attorney fees and lease the place back to them with a much lower rent than their current mortgage.

Instead of facing years of mounting legal bills, stress and uncertainty, which will only culminate in a credit-destroying foreclosure and eventual eviction, I can make all those problems go away right now. They don't have to move and disrupt their life. I can even sweeten the pot by tossing in an immediate cash bonus. Turning their crippling debt into a quick nest egg.

Now, I know what you're thinking at this point. "Why would I want a tenant with such a poor payment history?" And it's true. The unfortunate reality is that most homeowners who are unable or unwilling to pay their mortgage are not going to pay their rent, even if the price goes down significantly.

If they do keep paying on time and in full, great. That rent is mostly profit for you, since your holding costs are next to nothing. You'll likely recover your paltry initial investment in just a few months too. And you still have plenty of options for a big "pay day" down the road, since you can negotiate a short payoff with the bank, wholesale to another rental-focused investor or even buy back the property at a discount during the foreclosure auction.

However, far too often, the owner winds up defaulting within just two or three months of starting the new lease. You've done what you could to help, but it's time to cancel the lease and activate your writ of possession. Depending on how stringent the eviction laws in your state are, you should have the home clear and ready to sale on the market within a few months. In my online course, I cover the legal minutia of how to safely structure these lease back deals and head off problems in advance.

Homeowner wants to sell but lacks the financial means to relocate.

Solution: This is one of those ideal scenarios that lets you negotiate in relation to what the owner needs, rather than just against your best offer. In this situation, usually the owner has more pressing debt than the mortgage, so they're willing to "leave some money on the table" if it means getting quick cash.

So let's say your research gives you a top line offer on a property at $30k. You plan on opening with $15k and then negotiate from there. However, once you start talking to the prospect and get a sense of their life situation, you realize they're really motivated to sell. For example, when they keep asking about how fast this process takes. So instead of a traditional negotiation, you dig deeper and ask them exactly what obstacles are in the way of them moving out. Then you tally those expenses up with the client.

They'll need a security deposit for their new place, plus first and last months' rent. We should also get a moving company to speed things up. And what about their car payments? Are they behind? In most places in America, having your auto repossessed is even worse than foreclosure. How are they going to get to work?

So together you've added up an easy $10k in expenses. Then you mention you can handle that. Even top it off with another $5k in walking around money so the owner can celebrate and treat their family to a little vacation. And naturally, you'll cover all closing costs.

Now your "low ball" offer seems incredibly generous. Too good to pass up. After all, this is still a win-win situation for everyone. Maybe they could hold out for a better deal, but no one understands their problems better than you. And you're offering to make all their troubles go away, to change their life, *today*. You'll have the paperwork finished and the cash in their pocket in just 48 hours. That's the type of pitch that moves them into fast action. Even if a new investor comes along and offers them $20k, it's hard for most people to back away from an immediate payoff for the promise of a slightly higher one in the future.

Owner suggests some sort of alternative financing/purchasing scheme.

This is a slam dunk if you're willing to take title through a QCD, but when you're first starting out, you might not be ready to do that yet.

If you're wholesaling by assignment, then you need a regular, old fashioned "as is" purchase agreement. Anything else, no matter how great the numbers are on paper, will be hard sell to any 3rd party buyer.

So focus on the troubles they currently have that your offer will resolve and how fast you can close, rather than whatever complicated plan the seller is proposing. If they insist, then treat them as a reluctant seller. Tell them you'll check with your investor network and "What's your email? So I can forward any information from interested buyers your way?"

Keep following up though, since you'll usually find that their hopes have been shattered after a week or two and they're more interested in a regular sale.

Owner tries to start a bidding war.

Even though you've moved faster than most investors and agents, the owner has been pro-actively reaching out to various distressed property buyers and just wants to know your top-line offer. Any number you quote, they call back soon with a real or imagined offer from someone else that's always just a little higher than yours.

Solution: Boy, oh boy, I've been caught in the crossfire of countless bidding wars. Especially when a homeowner is actively seeking out offers and everyone swarms on this new "hot" lead. In this environment, it's so easy for otherwise cool and calm professionals to get sucked into the game and make emotionally charged mistakes. So when you hear the first shots fired, you need to stay rock-solid neutral. You're Switzerland, quietly getting rich while everyone else is duking it out and losing money, even when they win a war.

Once you realize you're dealing with a serious, well-informed customer, then give your best offer and stick to it, no matter what.

Once the homeowner notices you standing firm on your price, they'll try all sorts of things to tempt you. A savvy negotiator will attempt to push your buttons and make you second-guess yourself. "You know, how confident are you in your estimate of my home's value? Isn't that a conservative guess anyway? If you could just budge a *little* on your top offer, we could make this deal happen right now and you'll still make plenty of money."

That might sound reasonable, but a little is never enough. If you up your price a half-percentage point, they'll ask for a full point tomorrow. And another, and yet another. Soon, you're way past your tolerance level, but you're also so close to sealing the deal. You've invested so much time already, and just maybe you were being too pessimistic in your valuation...

No. Just. Don't.

Don't rationalize anything. Don't second-guess yourself. When I hear the drums of a bidding war brewing or any other wild stories from a homeowner, that's when my empathy fades. All that goes through my head is "Yadda yadda." Once I know I'm dealing with a savvy lead who has time for games, it's time to show them that I don't have any free play time. My standard response is:

"I understand you, but please realize my partner is an active buyer with multiple investment projects in the works. I've closed many purchases with them, and I can assure you they will not deviate from the budget under any circumstances. So what I'm offering you is the best price we can manage. I can lock the rate in place for 48 hours, but after that we'll have to lower the price, since the available equity in your property is shrinking fast as foreclosure approaches. If you're interested, I can prepare all the terms and forms for you to review and email that to you by the morning."

If the deal is really attractive, I'll follow up a few days later to sniff the air and see if anything's changed, but that's it. It's important to stand by everything you say. You make the best good faith offer you can tolerate and don't bother with any games. Ignore the bluffs and just lay your cards on the table. Otherwise, you're no longer an angel investor and you become just another run of the mill salesperson.

A married couple hold joint title. One wants to take your offer, but the other doesn't.

Perhaps even made more complicated if the relationship is on the rocks and one spouse has moved out.

Solutions: Ideally, we would have avoided this issue in the filtering leads phase by focusing on Lis Pendens with only a single defendant. Generally, you want to deal with as few interested parties as possible, but sometimes you'll see a home with so much equity baked in that you're willing to take on these additional complications.

Yes, at the end of the day the couple is just going to have to work out the decision on their own, but there are a few things we can do to help. If it's just a typical domestic squabble, we learn the holdout's end game. Find out what he or she wants most of all and how can we make that happen, just like with the previous responses. Needless to say, it's important to stay aloof, focusing on solutions and not give them the impression you're agreeing or disagreeing with their partner.

If the couple is in the process of divorcing, then it should be even easier to convince them to sell fast. Ask to speak with their lawyers. I know that sounds weird, but I love dealing with lawyers. Maybe I lose a little profit on the margins, but I know that things will go much smoother and faster. Plus, I have a new partner in the deal that will pressure their client to accept my "generous" offer. You always need to focus on the big picture to survive and thrive in the long run.

Owner has long since moved away and stopped paying the mortgage, while renting the home out.

Perhaps even on a long-term lease. The unfortunate renter has no idea the property is facing foreclosure.

Solution: This is definitely a mixed-blessing situation. On the downside, you're buying the lease and its associated responsibilities (i.e. baggage) as well as the deed. And unlike when you're leasing back a property to the original owner, the current tenant has no particular motivation to keep the home well maintained. They're not getting any extra money out of the deal. On the plus side, the absentee owner is usually far less attached to the property and more amenable to a discounted sell. In addition, the tenant has probably been vetted and is far less likely to default.

Still, as long as you respect the terms of the lease and you have a strong foreclosure defense strategy, then you can treat this just like an HOA foreclosure. Explain the situation to your new tenant. They might not be sympathetic, but you have nothing to lose by treating them with respect. Make sure you get them on a month-to-month lease as soon as you can. Adding a little extra to the security deposit, paid out of your own pocket, can always go a long way to ensuring a smooth transition for the tenant. Again, don't lose sight of the big picture over a grand or two of petty cash.

Probate Common Objections and Responses:

It's not my property yet, it's my (deceased relative).

> I understand. According to our records, you'll soon be the probate administrator, giving you authority to sell the property and disburse the proceeds. That's why we pay in all cash upfront without requiring a property inspection or anything else. We want to make this process as fast and simple as possible. When would be a good time to sit down and discuss all the options?

I don't know if we're going to sell the house... (or general indecisiveness/noncommittal to any course of action).

> Of course, I've been there. So much to consider. Well, our investor network is quite large. We have many options that could take the decision pressure off of you. For example, if you want to

rent the property out, we can find you high-quality tenants and handle all the details of property management. When would be a good time to sit down and discuss all the options?

I'd like to sell immediately, but (other family member) wants (something else).

> No worries. I can help with that. If you send me this person's phone number, I'll be happy to discuss all the details with them so you don't have to worry about it. I've never come across a case where we haven't been able to work out a win-win situation for everyone involved.

I'd like to sell, but I (or another) family member is currently living there and can't afford/doesn't want to move out.

> Not a problem. We're quite flexible and have many different options. For example, we could offer to lease the property back to the current occupant, while still providing everyone a sizeable upfront cash payment for the lease. When would be a good time to sit down and discuss all the options?

What's this lowball offer? I'm not selling for less than... (any attempt to negotiate price).

> I hear you. Well, I have many investors in my network, each with different budgets and goals, so let me ask around. In the meantime, I'm happy to show you my cost and value estimates, so you can see how potential buyers arrive at their max purchase price. Even if you wind up selling to someone else, this report should come in quite handy to make sure you get the best price possible. What email address should I send it to?

They don't have the slightest interest in a cash offer. Savvy seller that wants to take the property to the broad market.

Actually, that's a great idea. While I can't offer you what you want, I have a close working relationship with a great listing agent that specializes in your neighborhood. They can get you top dollar on the property while still selling it fast. When would be a good time to have them call you?

Key Follow Up Questions Before Sending The Contract

So you've been on the phone for a while, maybe even multiple calls over days, and the buyer is warmed up and ready to receive your written offer. Now it's time to ask a few fishing questions so you can perform your final due diligence and send that purchase contract with confidence.

1) *Do they have a contract with a listing agent already? If so, what type of listing agreement do they have?*

    This isn't usually a problem, since the property is off market, but some really proactive folks going through probate or pre-foreclosure might have signed with an agent but not yet listed the property. If they have an agent, we'll need their name and contact info so we can work out an arrangement.

2) *How's the property condition? Are you aware of any issues, such as mold, termites, leaking roof, broken appliances/doors/windows, that sort of thing? What do you think is necessary to get this up to ready-to-rent standards? Again, we'll handle all the repairs. Nothing you have to worry about. We just want to get an initial idea of how much we should budget so this whole process goes smoothly.*

    Take note of whatever they say, but this self-assessment is far from accurate... to put things charitably. The only reason we ask this question is to ease them into the next question, which is far more important. Now that they've told some white lies about their property and glossed over unpleasant details, they're naturally inclined to be more open about the positive things:

3) *Have there been any renovations, repairs or improvements to the property? Anything that might increase the property's value since it was built?*

   a) Here's where they're happy to brag. Especially if they mentioned a few negative points in the last question. Document everything just in case, but we don't care much about the little stuff. New appliances, flooring, paint job, et al aren't going to change your max purchase price.

   b) We're looking for major things that require building permits. You need to research what needs permitting in your local area, of course, but some of the most common things to be on the lookout for are:

      i) New attached structures, like patios, garages, pools.

      ii) Extensive electrical or plumbing work.

      iii) New rooms, stories, chimneys, sky roofs, any roofing activity.

      iv) Renovations that change the "living space" square footage, at least for tax purposes. For example, converting the garage to a den, attics to bedrooms, or a "Florida room" (enclosed patio) into an air conditioned/heated living room.

   c) This is very important in our risk assessment phase, because we'll compare what work they say has been done with what has been recorded at the tax collector's and code enforcement websites. Too often you'll find that the owner never got a permit for the work, which means hefty fees for code violations, inspections and usually additional repairs to fix the sloppy work done by the likely unlicensed contractor.

   None of this is a deal breaker though. We can adjust our offer to compensate for all of these issues, but the last thing in the world we want is for our end buyer to be surprised.

These violations are also a useful bit of leverage to push a reluctant seller over the finish line, since in a traditional sale they would have to give a massive price credit or pay to get all these things fixed before a bank will lend money to the buyer. They now have an easy choice to make:

Refuse our offer and come up with the (significant) cash to fix these issues before selling on the open market, or take a slightly lower offer and not spend a dime. And let's face it, if they had the money and time to bring their property to market, they would have done so already.

4) *Who's currently living in the property? What are their lease terms? If owner occupied, how long do they need to move out?*

You'll also need them to send you a copy of the rental lease when you sign the purchase contract. If your jurisdiction requires any tenant notifications prior to a sale, then make sure the seller knows this. Send them a pre-written letter/form that they just have to sign. Which makes it easier for the seller and gives you piece of mind the documentation was filled out correctly.

If owner occupied, offer to cover any moving expenses (credited against the price, of course.) Anything you can do to solve their problems and make things easy increases the chances you'll close the deal.

5) *Do you know of any outstanding liens, mortgages, lawsuits or anything like that against the property? I just want to make sure we'll be paying off everything that's owed at closing.*

Again, you'll double check the court records before signing the contract, but if they don't even know how much they owe on the property, then that's going to cause all sorts of problems if they stay in the dark until closing. Sometimes, especially with inherited properties, you'll be the first person explaining to the owner how many liens there are on the place. Besides giving you some negotiating leverage, you're also building trust and confidence with the seller.

Full transparency helps everything move forward smoothly and is *never* an obstacle. For example, say the owner is happy to sell for

$150k because they think they only owe $140k on the property. But if you know there's another $15k in liens that they're forgetting about, it might be tempting to stay quiet. Otherwise they'll want to raise the price to at least $155k. Don't fall for this temptation, because the truth will come out eventually and they'll do everything they can to scuttle the deal at the last second. Maybe even damage the property out of spite. Being fully transparent and honest will always save you time, money and stress in the long run.

6) *Do they own any other properties? Is there any way you can help with them?*

Remember that your local records search generally only covers one county. What if they own another property out of town or even out of state? One red flag is if the property is not listed as a homestead in the tax rolls. Knowing more about their situation opens the door to close multiple deals at once, or at least offer more options with the current deal.

For a common example, say someone took out a reverse mortgage on their primary residence to purchase an investment property. For some reason that investment is not paying off and they're now facing foreclosure on their family home that they can't or won't move away from. In this situation, the seller isn't interested in saving some of their equity, they just want to save their main home and stop the foreclosure as fast as possible.

So learning more gives you a chance to pay off just what they owe, saving you and the end buyer a lot. Not to mention that you'll receive unique insights into any unknown challenges with renting or flipping in the area that wouldn't be readily apparent otherwise.

Post-Contact But Pre-Signing Due Diligence

Regardless of the responses to this due diligence risk assessment, you have to be able to answer all of these questions if you want end buyers to gobble up your contract fast. Again, negative information on a property is never a problem. Just a variable that changes the price, but unknown risk factors can break deals.

- ✓ Any HOA/COA involved? Do they have any weird by-laws that could disrupt rental plans? For example, a rule stating that short-term (Airbnb style) rentals aren't allowed. The bylaws are usually recorded at your local courthouse/land records, but in many cases it's easier to just call or email the association manager and ask them.

- ✓ Occupancy. Who is in the property right now? If owner-occupied, how long do they need to move out? If a tenant, get a copy of the lease and find out if the renter is current on their payments.

- ✓ If vacant, is the power off or on? You can ask the homeowner, but you can usually double check this with the start service feature on the website of the local power company.

- ✓ Who's currently handling maintenance/upkeep? The owner, the tenant, the HOA, a property management company or no one? If the owner/tenant or no one, then you can budget for more rehab and staging work.

- ✓ Outstanding tax balance. This is usually available on the property appraiser's website or on the tax assessor's separate website.

- ✓ Double check every single detail of the property's description. You'll already be doing most of this when you look for code violations, so take five more minutes to finish what you started. Go line by line through the Zillow page and any past MLS listings and compare each data point to the tax assessor's records. You should make a note of every single discrepancy in your report. Even if it's inconsequential to the deal, you don't want the buyer to discover an error on their own and then doubt your professionalism and thoroughness.

- ✓ Unofficial title search. The end buyer is going to pay for the full title search and insurance at closing, but you still need to doublecheck the basics to make sure the seller can provide that general warranty deed. You've done most of this already when you tallied up all the liens on the property, so the main things you're looking for now are:

- Any other title owners that need to sign the purchase agreement that you haven't talked to yet? Such as a spouse not listed on the mortgage or another heir in probate.

- Will the final sale price be enough to satisfy all lien holders? Including the extra attorney/court/back interest fees to satisfy the foreclosure? Never be tempted to say, "Well, that's not my problem." It will become your problem later. The seller will assume you're taking advantage of them and try every creative way they can imagine to get out of the deal. Even if that means damaging the property.

- Are there any pending or recently closed judgments that haven't yet been recorded as liens? Budget for them as well.

- Are there any deed restrictions or other encumbrances besides liens? For example, private easements or encroachments by neighbors. Deed restrictions limiting land use, riparian rights already sold off to a 3rd party, etc…

✓ Known and potential code and zoning violations: (see next section).

Recognizing Potential Code Violations.

Here we're not so worried about nuisance violations, like overgrown weeds or piles of trash in the yard. If there's an active fine for that type of stuff, we'll deduct the costs from our offer price. If they haven't been fined yet, we'll warn the buyer about the potential issue, which rarely becomes a problem because they can clean these problems up fast after closing.

But one major potential landmine with flipping or wholesaling off-market properties is the unknown risk of local building code violations. Primarily unpermitted renovations.

Sure, sometimes there might be an unpaid judgment or even lien on the property by the city, but most of the time these issues exist only as potential violations at the moment.

These are the types of things your buyer's GC might not notice in an as-is condition off-market transaction, but these issues won't stay hidden for long. When the property is eventually sold on the open market and it's being scrutinized by underwriters for the new buyer's lender, that's when these surprises tend to come out.

For example, maybe a renovation was done quite professionally, so there's nothing amiss you'd notice in a walkthrough. But was there a permit required for that work? If the investor knows about this ahead of time, they can get these issued fixed and up to code quite cheaply.

But if they didn't know about this until after they bought from you, invested their own cash into rehab and then they're suddenly getting hit with an expensive code violation days before closing... who do you think they're going to blame?

This is someone who has already bought from you, so by definition one of your best clients. You want to keep this relationship going for years and have them recommend you to all their friends and family. So that means while maybe you aren't legally liable for any potential code violations, your all-important reputation is most definitely on the line.

That's why it's so important to go the extra mile and make searching for unpermitted renovations/repairs an integral part of your due diligence. It only takes a few minutes to flag these potential problems, all without ever getting inside the property.

1. Are there any discrepancies among the property details between the property appraiser website and past listings on Zillow or the MLS? For example, if the tax man lists the property as having 2,000 sq ft and an online listing mentions 2100, then that's a huge red flag the owner might have done some unpermitted renovations that your buyer will be on the hook for.

   Something as minor as one site mentioning a half bath and another a full bath is worth noting. Even if there are no code violations involved, it's important to flag this for your end buyer. If you don't know why there is a discrepancy, then just say so in your buyer's report.

2. Look up the known permits from the appropriate county website and compare that list to what the homeowner says has been done. Mention every discrepancy in your report, even if it's unlikely to be fineable.

3. Check the local code enforcement website and court judgments for any open, unpaid fines. Remember, in many cases these violations aren't filed as liens on the property. If the records aren't available online, there's usually no problem just calling the local code enforcement office. Tell them you're planning on purchasing a property at __ and ask if there are any past or pending permits, or unpaid fines.

Remember: You don't have to determine if something is a violation, only disclose anything that *might* be an issue. It's actually a great thing if the buyer thinks you're a "Nervous Nancy" who's worrying about nothing.

So list all known building permits for the property, and contrast them with what the tax assessor's website says and what you heard from the seller or seen yourself. Many of these are going to be false flags, but the buyer will feel more confident that you did your homework and you're being transparent.

How To Get Out Of Those Bidding Wars.

While you might have been the first investor to reach out, you won't be the last. And despite the research you put into your offer, someone can always top it. Sometimes a direct cash investor will swoop in, and they'll always be able to outgun a wholesaler's bid.

More often though, this better offer is coming from some new, inexperienced wholesaler who's promising something they can't deliver. Of course, you can't convince the seller of that. They'll just have to find out the hard way, a month or so down the road when the deal never closes.

So whether you're bidding against someone with a legitimately higher acquisition budget or someone peddling fantasy, either way you're fighting a war you can't win. There's no upside for you, but plenty of risk.

So don't even get involved.

If you followed my advice, your initial offer was close to your max offer. You have a little flexibility to make some concessions to the seller so they feel better about the deal, but not enough room to effectively bid against other parties. Once you hit your top-line price, stick to your guns no matter what. Be casual and friendly about it, we want them to remember us as their number 1 back up offer, but stay firm.

Don't be tempted to second guess your CMA or ARV. There's a big subjective element to any real estate analysis, which can trip you up in a hurry. When the lead exists simply as some data on a spreadsheet, it's easy to be neutral in your evaluation. But when the seller is on the phone and "oh so eager to make this happen today," it's harder to stay impartial.

You can taste your profit already and there are countless ways to manipulate the data, even subconsciously, into returning the numbers you want to see.

So instead of running the numbers again, go over them with the seller. Show them your comps and how you arrived at the ARV. Explain how an investor evaluates such deals and how much they must pay for rehab, staging, carrying and closing costs. Prove that your top offer is based on non-negotiable reality, rather than some number you pulled out of your hat.

Even if this fails to build trust and they're skeptical of your math, you're still knocking them off guard and giving them food for thought. I guarantee giving away your "trade secrets" was the last thing the seller expected as a counteroffer.

Risk Management - Key Clauses In The Wholesale Contract

Right to Assignment

By default, residential real estate purchase agreements are assignable in just about every situation. To avoid any confusion though, make sure the assignment clause is clearly spelled out and labeled. Don't just mention "and/or assigns" after your name or bury it in the fine print, in other words. Outside of the contract, the seller should be fully aware that you are not the end buyer. There's no need to make this complicated though. Simply explain that: "One of my partners will be providing the cash to purchase. Since I've worked with them in the past, I know they can close on your property fast."

Right to Show

This isn't absolutely necessary, but one of those "nice to haves" and pretty easy to get if the property is vacant. Your end buyer will appreciate that they have the right to show the property to prospective tenants or buyers before closing.

All the disclosures.

Again, there are countless additional clauses/forms that cities and counties might require in local real estate transactions. Most of these are mere formalities... unless you forget to include them. Just pay your attorney the miniscule fees required to prep a template contract for your local area and you'll never have to worry about any fines.

This sounds so elementary, but I've seen too many wholesalers just download some purchase agreement from the internet and don't have a clue how much liability they're exposing themselves to.

Contingencies:

There's no need for a bunch of special contingency clauses to weasel out of the contract if things go south. Afterall, you'll know within 24 hours if your buyers are interested in the deal. There might be some last-minute haggling over your assignment fee, but if you can't get them to sign the Assignment Agreement, or at least get their contractor to inspect the property, within 72 hours, then they just aren't interested. For example, if the buyer really wanted the property but needs a few weeks to free up cash or secure financing, they would still sign the agreement and put down a deposit to lock in the contract first.

This is rarely a problem if you've invested even a little effort into estimating the buyer's costs and the property's realistic ARV. Because then you know you have a marketable contract, even if you have to drop your fee a tad to sweeten the deal.

If for some reason your estimates were so far off that reducing your assignment fee isn't enough to convince buyers to close, it's good to know this fast. While you're still covered by the regular inspection period clause. In which case, you need to notify the seller ASAP to get your earnest money deposit back and free them up to accept other offers. Don't waste everyone's time using all of that 15-day inspection window shopping the deal around to less experienced buyers. Just back out fast. That's the fair thing to do for the distressed seller, as well as the most efficient use of your time.

Again though, finding yourself with an unmarketable contract will be a rare problem, because price is a risk factor that you have total control over. However, there are three risk items that are out of your control, so we want to make sure there's a contingency clause for each:

Inspection clause

Always include at least a two-week inspection period clause in your offer. Yes, you're purchasing "as is" and at a steep discount, so you're not going to have much luck trying to get credits for repairs. Nonetheless, you need this escape clause to protect you and the end buyer from any massive physical defects with the property that could wipe out all the equity in the deal.

A lot of wholesalers don't want to mention the inspection period in their prospectus. That's because they're marketing to any random buyer and don't want to waste their time showing the house to dozens of unmotivated buyers. But this won't be a problem for you, since you're dealing with only the most motivated buyers.

Documentation clause

This gives you the right to back out if the seller can't provide crucial documentation within a reasonable time frame for your title agent to arrange closing. For example, if there's a tenant in the property and the seller is dragging their feet about getting you a copy of the lease agreement.

Court approval (for probates)

This simple clause has a large time window, usually three months. It gives the seller time to petition the court to approve the sale, but also protects you if the court takes forever or some other problem arises with the estate.

Phase IV – Finding and Working with End Buyers

Locating And Qualifying Cash Buyers Fast

You should build your list of buyers before you start reaching out to clients, but even if that's not how things worked out in practice, you can still hunt them down fast. And yes, if you have a quality deal under contract, then finding someone to buy it is the easiest part of this whole process. You could just check out recent sales in the neighborhood that were bought by an LLC or start hitting up multi-property owners on the tax rolls to find buyers.

However, if you want to scale this wholesaling business up and spend the bulk of your time feeding properties into the pipeline, then you need a list of vetted buyers so you can finish the sale fast. This isn't a listing contract you can sit on for months, but rather a firm purchase contract with a short shelf life. Not to mention that you promised the seller you could close on the property within five days. If you don't deliver on your promise, they have every right to torpedo the deal. And the longer it takes to close, the more all those back up offers they're getting will tempt them.

Which is why you can't do business with just any random buyer off the street. Not if you're looking for long-term, reliable and scalable success. You're running a professional wholesaling business here, so you don't have time to deal with amateur investors. You need other pros as partners. In an ideal scenario, you want to assign the contract to a buyer the same day you signed with the seller. Basically the same as a double close, but without the closing costs. Even if that means you're not fetching the highest price. Remember, the real money comes from how fast you can turn over inventory, rather than eking out every penny in a deal.

So once again, in order to make this dream come true and generate steady profits on a regular basis, you need quality buyers. The type of soon-to-be partners that check all of the following boxes:

1. They have plenty of cash on hand or a private lending source to close on your deal right now. Obviously, you don't have the time to wait on someone to secure traditional financing, nor do you want some 4th party complicating things.

2. They're actively seeking new inventory right now. They aren't looking to buy next month or next quarter, but the money is burning a hole in their pocket today. You're bringing them ultra-motivated sellers, so you should only be dealing with ultra-motivated buyers.

3. Most important of all: They must have experience purchasing and rehabbing distressed properties that are bought off the MLS. We want to deal with confident off-market investors that have done this before and won't get cold feet when it's time to close.

Ok, I realize that a lot of readers are going to snicker and roll their eyes at this point, because it sounds like I'm shrinking the potential pool of buyers into a tiny, elite group. After all, shouldn't you be trying to cast as wide a net as possible? More potential buyers equal faster closing and higher assignment fees, right? All the pros say I should be posting on Craigslist or running PPC ads or some other form of mass marketing...

After all the time, money and stress you've spent researching and securing a great wholesale deal, you can't play games now. You want to keep that pipeline flowing without any bottlenecks. You can't waste your time with inexperienced, nervous buyers that are at a high risk of leaving you hanging at closing.

So to do this right, you need to focus on the highest quality buyer leads in the same way you targeted the highest quality seller leads.

But the good news is that once you start hunting down these top-notch buyers, you'll find that they aren't so rare. There are so many of these choice investors hiding in plain sight. And you can find them fast in just about every market by looking at two sources:

1) Auction winners.

If you aren't familiar with them already, take a minute to look up where foreclosure and tax sale auctions are held in your county. Usually this is done through the local courthouse, though sometimes via the sheriff's office or hosted by a 3rd party service. Even in the 21st century, occasionally the auctions aren't conducted online and are still held "on the courthouse steps," like the Wild West (Fun times. That's where I got my start in real estate).

In any case, there are public records of who won these auctions and who is bidding at current auctions. What you're looking for are the winning bidders for past auctions, who are also actively placing bids at the current auction. Specifically, anyone who has:

- Won at least one auction this year. The more, the better.
- Actually took title to what they purchased. You'll be surprised how many folks win an auction but fail to come up with enough cash to finalize the purchase.
- Is still bidding on more properties this month.

Generally this is as simple as creating an auction bidder account yourself to monitor past results and current auctions. Sometimes the bidder names are hidden and you have to search for the Certificate of Title by the property address at the register of deed's office. But it doesn't matter how hard it is to track these auction winners down, because it's worth the effort. These "risk-on" buyers will be your most loyal clients. If you have any trouble, shoot me an email and I'll put my research team on the case. No charge if you mention that you read this book.

Anyway, this list of active and successful auction bidders is solid gold for a wholesaler, since all your vetting is already done. And then some:

1. These auction winners have cash on hand and a proven track record of spending it fast on off-market deals. In just about every auction, winning bids have to be settled 100% in cash within 24 hours. So if they're actively bidding, they've got some free cash in their account. Plus, it's such a breath of fresh air when a

wholesaler comes along offering a couple of days to close, and even allows an inspection!

2. They deal with some of the most distressed properties out there, so besides being experienced buyers, the inventory you're bringing them is automatically high quality. Even if the property requires extensive rehab, simply getting that clean general warranty deed instead of a dirty certificate of title adds significant value to the deal.

3. They understand exactly how you're sourcing your leads and how you determined your value and pricing. Afterall, these auction investors are poring over the exact same court cases as you are, just later in the process. They have the same dataset and similar process for calculating equity at a distance, and they've been dreaming of reaching the homeowner before an auction was scheduled. In short, you two are speaking the same language.

4. They are less risk adverse. Auction winners are happy to hear you out and are far more likely to see the value a wholesaler brings to the table. Expect them to ask direct and in-depth questions that you might not have the answer for immediately and have to look it up. But unlike retail buyers, they won't consider dealing with you to be inherently riskier than their current business model.

Look at it from their prospective. While auctions are quite lucrative, buying foreclosed properties with "dirty" title blind at auction is also the most competitive and riskiest way to build inventory. I've bought hundreds of properties at auction. I've even been burned a few times, yet I'm still placing bids every week in my favorite counties. Maybe I'm addicted to the rush, but nonetheless I also know from experience that buying from a wholesaler is far safer than at an auction. Which is why it's so easy for you wholesalers to convert us auction winners.

Come on, we're just begging for you to come and take our money. Bring us a clean title deal that's got some halfway decent equity in it and we're putty in your hands. Now, we will probe you and your deals more thoroughly than any proctologist, but if you deliver what you promised on a regular basis, you'll be our go-to guy or gal. Then you can mark up the price and set any terms and conditions you like.

2) Active flippers.

This is where the local property appraiser site will come in handy. We're not looking for someone that recently bought a foreclosure off market, since they'll be less interested in a new deal until that one is complete and they have free capital to play with. Instead, we're looking for those investors who have just successfully flipped a property for a tidy profit and are likely looking for another deal fast.

You'll want to search by recent sales and filter for those properties that:

1. Were both bought and sold within a 3-6 month time span in the same area as your subject. This is a general rule of thumb to identify experienced flippers, but it does vary depending on the average time on market in your area. So use properties flipped in this time frame as the hottest source of buyers to contact, but don't ignore deals taking place outside of this time range.

   Generally, if the flip went down too fast (less than 90 days), the investor is probably either only looking for turn-key ready properties, or they had some problem that forced them to sell fast. So there's a good chance they're either too picky or too inexperienced for your purposes and should be a lower priority to contact.

   If it took longer than six months to flip, then likely they're most interested in fixer upper properties, and so will expect a great deal from you, or they made some mistake that took them longer to flip, which will make them more risk adverse with their next deal. Either way, they're a lower priority contact for most wholesale deals.

2. The original purchase was for a pre-foreclosure or another problematic off-market sale. This is to make sure they're experienced with rehabbing distressed properties.

3. The flip sale was completed in the last month. The sooner, the better. We want to get to them before they put their money back to work.

Note: when I say "bought," remember that many experienced flippers are first taking title to properties via a quit claim deed, then negotiating settlements with creditors before reselling on the open market. So you're looking for all types of title transfers to identify flippers, and not only traditional sales.

Since commercial real estate sites like Zillow or the MLS usually don't count quit claim deeds in sales reports, the best way to spot these title transfers is by checking the recent sales at your local property appraiser's office. When you see a QCD on a parcel number, followed by a regular sale (with a warranty deed) on that folio number a few months later, you're likely looking at an experienced flipper. With the added bonus that they recently flipped a property in the same neighborhood as your subject property and would like to repeat their success.

Approaching these investors at any time is smart, but if you can find them right after a successful sale, then you can add extra value. Because at this point, they're likely sitting on a pile of cash and looking to put it to work. Flippers are just like you and know it's all about how fast they can turn over inventory. Since so many take advantage of 1031 exchanges to put off their tax payments, they're also under a time crunch. They now have just 45 days to identify a replacement investment.

While there are several ways to qualify for the 1031 exchange, the most common approach is the IRS's "Three properties" rule. Here the investor can replace one property with three other investments, assuming they identify them within 45 days and close within 180. Which is a great program, but it does require a steady flow of new inventory to work.

I can't tell you how many times I've had a bumper month flipping properties... but then the real stress began. I couldn't take my time to handle all my due diligence and had to figure out how to replace those five flips last month with 15 new investments this month before Uncle Sam came to collect his pound of flesh. If only some savvy wholesaler was on hand with a package of gift-wrapped investments that I could close on immediately...

Introducing Yourself To New Cash Buyers

Ok, so you've built your potential buyer list. Unless you have a deal handy right now, you need to warm them up first.

As a completely unknown wholesaler, it's unlikely you're going to get a letter of intent to invest or even any firm verbal interest when you first contact these folks. They've seen too many sketchy operators promising the moon, so don't expect any serious engagement until you bring them a contract with serious equity in the deal. In other words, you have to "put up or shut up."

Still, it's not a waste of time to make your introductions to these potential cash buyers well before you bring them a deal. Be ultra-transparent and explain how you source your leads and contact sellers, as well as any special niches you focus on or past experience you bring to the table.

Make it clear that you aren't selling anything at the moment, but just introducing yourself and your company. Naturally, they're going to want to see proof that you can actually get these properties under contract at well below market rates, but you will pique their curiosity in the meantime. This is all such a fresh take that you will definitely stand out.

And remember, warming up buyers is not a one-time thing. As you're working your seller list, show off your data and send a few free leads to your potential buyers. When a seller turns you down, just send that "dead" lead to any prospective buyer you want to build a relationship with. Cut and paste directly from your Excel sheet and share everything you know about the property, including the skip-traced phone numbers.

Just like with sellers, if your follow up is offering some type of value, then it's not really a follow up message. You're still working a long-term soft sale.

Even better, trust is in dreadfully short supply in the real estate business, so sharing your property data is guaranteed to make an impression. And don't worry if they run with the lead and buy the property. This is data you would have thrown away otherwise. Now you can "recycle" the leads. It doesn't cost you anything. Fresh distressed seller court filings are a renewable resource for you. Let's hope the potential buyer does profit fast from your data. Now that they know your leads are red-hot, they'll be begging you for more.

And next time you'll be bringing them a locked down contract ready for assignment and immediate closing.

What To Ask Your Potential End Buyers.

Asking what areas they want to invest in or what types of property they're looking for is a total waste of time. As a real estate pro, you should know which neighborhoods are hot and what's not (remember the time on market screening in the CMA section?). And as for property type... who cares? All that matters is how much profit the deal has in it.

Yeah, most investors will say they're looking for "multi-unit properties," but if you bring them a single family home in a popular area with at least 30% equity in the deal, that's within their price range, you can bet they'll figure out a way to adapt and overcome. Don't forget, you aren't dealing with the meek and humble, but rather the greediest capitalists America's high-octane real estate market attracts.

In practice, there are only three things you need to know from your prospective buyers when you're first reaching out:

1) What's your budget this month? Assuming each is a high-equity deal, how much are you willing to allot to cash deals this month? How much with hard money leverage?

2) What's your preferred investment strategy at the moment? For example, acquiring income-producing properties, quick flips or longer fix and flips?

3) Do you have any special pet peeves? Any particular types of deals you're not interested in, no matter the discount?

Later, after you've developed a closer relationship, you can ask for more specific details so you can bring them deals they'll pay top dollar for. But for the initial research, this gives you enough information to estimate your max acquisition price for different types of properties and who to send the contracts to.

For example, properties that can generate the highest rent and need the least rehab are going to be more expensive to acquire from the seller. A flipper is going to be less interested in them, but someone looking for long-term rental properties would pay a premium for these contracts.

And those properties that we're getting the cheapest but also have the highest rehab costs? Your fix and flippers will love them. They already have a way to cut their repair costs. Now they need you to reduce the acquisition costs.

As for everything in between, that's the bread and butter inventory for quick flippers. Investors looking for a quick flip want a compromise between quality and price, and specifically focus on how fast they can turn the property around.

How To Get Fast Engagement For Your Deal.

I've added a sample wholesaler property prospectus in the next section. While this is detailed, it doesn't need to be complicated.

The number one rule is full transparency. Show the buyer everything you've learned about the property, even and especially if it's negative. Full disclosure might break a particular deal, but that's small potatoes. It will cement your reputation as a thorough and reliable wholesaler, which will unlock more opportunities in the future.

And truth be told, bad news about a property is rarely a disaster. That's why we're building in such a large equity safety cushion in the first place and working with just experienced investors.

These end buyers are expecting to invest serious money into a property to unlock its maximum resell price. They aren't going to be intimidated by a long list of needed repairs, but vague information like, "Needs some TLC" is going to turn them off.

What drives down the price isn't property deficiencies, but rather fear of the unknown. Some wholesalers are skeptical about this and think I'm being naive, but the reality is disclosing everything that hurts a property's value is going to save time by filtering out the indecisive buyers fast, while getting the motivated buyers to execute right now.

Since there's always an element of risk involved with an "as is" purchase, the less a buyer knows about the asset, the larger the equity cushion they need. But the more they know, even if it's bad stuff, the less wiggle room they need in the pricing to protect against unknowns.

Remember, you're dealing only with the most experienced cash buyers, so simply offering a contract with a wide price to ARV spread isn't going to wow them. This isn't their first rodeo. They've seen such pie-in-the-sky estimates a million times. Their first reaction will be along the lines of, "What's wrong with this picture? Why is it so cheap? What are you not telling me?"

Again, known issues aren't problems. They're simply variables in the investment calculus. Something you can compensate for by lowering your assignment fee, if need be, but at least you're collecting a fee. The unknown issues are what cause mistrust and keep you from earning any sort of profit.

So the more light you can shine on an investment, even if you're highlighting negative things, the more likely you will be able to close on the deal. Impress buyers by pulling back as much of the "fog of investing" as possible. There's a huge psychological difference between researching unknown issues on an investment and just double checking your work.

So feel free to add anything to this, but you aren't ready to approach a buyer until you can do all of the following:

✓ Don't just give your estimated ARV and the price. Include the reason the price is so low right after you mention it. Simply adding "Pre-Foreclosure" or "In Probate: Rep lives out of state" answers the buyer's top question and lends credibility to everything else you're saying.

✓ You have a video ready that's more than a walkthrough of the property. It also includes footage of every positive and negative feature you mentioned in the prospectus. If you want fast buy-in, then you need to be able to prove everything your saying.

✓ Have detailed answers to all the due diligence questions from Phase III.

Your Assignment Offer

This might be the most intimidating aspect of wholesaling, but it should be the fun part. To sell your contract to these experienced clients, you just have to prove your numbers. That's it. Simply drown your end buyers in data so they feel confident and then let their natural greed take over.

Now, it's perfectly acceptable to send your wholesale deal to everyone on your buyer's list at the same time... But you need to award the contract on a first-come, first-served basis. It's going to cause problems if you try to shop around the deal. This is wholesale real estate, not retail. If you quote one price in your prospectus and get several positive responses in short order, don't be tempted to take advantage of the increased demand. If you resend the same contract with a new, higher price, then you're going to irritate your prospective clients. Sure, maybe you can bid up the price for this particular deal, but don't expect them to even read the next offer you send.

If you believe your deal is so valuable that it can fetch a premium assignment fee, then just increase the total purchase price you send with the prospectus to cover your larger expected profit. If you misjudged demand, no problem. You can always lower your assignment fee later, but never raise the price after you've given it.

When you're ready to approach these buyers, there are really three things you need to send them first, before you can call and ask for a firm commitment:

1) The initial one-page summary, or "property prospectus." This is the most important item to get buyers interested. It's similar to a property listing on the MLS, but also includes the quick answers to an investor's most pressing risk management questions.

There are many ways to pretty this up, but at a minimum you should include:

- Embed or link to your walkthrough/virtual inspection video at the beginning.

- Details of the deal: The end buyer's price, rental value, ARV, CMV, any contingencies or contract stipulations. Note: price should be the final sale price, inclusive of your assignment fee and any traditional seller closing costs that the end buyer will be paying. For example, if the seller is receiving $180k, plus the buyer pays the outstanding tax balance and transaction taxes of $4k without proration, and you want to earn a $10k assignment fee, the price you quote the buyer is $194k.

- Property details & comps: Just the most important highlights here. You can include every little detail in your attached full property report.

- Due diligence: These are the quick answers to the first questions a buyer will ask. You only need to cover major repair/code/zoning/legal issues, occupancy status, HOA/COA concerns and tax liability. All the other details go in the full report. For example, you don't need to list all the landscaping problems, broken appliances, painting work, carpet replacing and drywall patching here. That's routine rehab.

Instead, list the really bad things like a leaky roof, significant foundation repairs, mold or code violations. Your price is going to be low enough that they'll still come out with a profit no matter what, but if they're not interested in extensive repair work, we need to weed them out fast. And if they are a fix and flipper, they'll be more comfortable with the deal now that they know what they're getting into. If you lead with the worst, everything after that seems easy in comparison.

2) Your full property report, which is just all of the raw notes you've gathered on the property. We're in a hurry to close now, so anything we can do to help the buyer make up their mind fast helps us. We want them to spend their time fact checking your work, rather than having to do original research. Even if they say no, then we can call

the next person on our list in minutes and not have to wait a day or two for a response.

At a minimum, you should include:

- The details of your CMA.
- Any lower quality comps you looked at and rejected.
- Answers to all your due diligence questions.
- Likely needed repairs and cost estimates.
- Known building permits.
- A list of all encumbrances that will be satisfied at closing and anything that will remain.
- Breakdown of seller/buyer closing costs.
- Breakdown of price, including your assignment fee.
- Estimated cash needed at closing.

3) All supporting documentation. The assignment agreement, deposit escrow instructions, purchase contract, copy of current tenant lease, and any supplemental disclosures/forms required. Ensure they have everything they need to execute the assignment agreement right then and there.

Sample Prospectus

Deal Details

Price: $196,000   [Embedded walkthrough video]

ARV: $245,000

- As-Is Current Market Value: $213,000
- Estimated Rent: $1,550 /mo, based upon last lease that expired on [date].
- Source: Recent Foreclosure/Probate/Civil Judgment [link to case number]
- Inspection period ends: [Date]
- Contract contingencies/other stipulations:
  Property in probate. Sale contingent on court approval before [date]. Case # 123455789 (hyperlink to courthouse website).

Property Details

Parcel #:	(Hyperlink)	Built:	
Address:		Sq Footage:	
Neighborhood:		Units/Beds/Baths:	
Property Type:		Other Major Features:	
Construction Type:		Interior condition	Heavy, average, light rehab needed
		Exterior condition	
Comp 1:	Address (Link to appraiser)	Sale Date/Price	Distance from subject
Comp 2:			
Comp 3:			

Due Diligence (see attached report for full details)

Known and potential issues: Owner built attached patio without permit. May require a code inspection.

Occupancy: Vacant for last month, power on.

HOA: $75/month, no short or long term rental restrictions.

Outstanding tax balance: $1,250 (included in sales price)

Final Thoughts And Encouragement

Now that you're excited and hopefully taken some notes to take your business to the next level, this is where I'm supposed to upsell you on my online courses and lead generation resources. Truth is, if you've read and applied everything in this book, the online resources are completely optional. This book has all the core fundamentals you need to kickstart you career way beyond the competition.

With that said, I can still offer you several resources to cut down the learning curve and give you a larger edge in any market.

1) The most popular tool is a monthly subscription to our lead generation service. This covers:

Tier 1 leads - Every new foreclosure and probate filings in your target county.

Tier 2 and some Tier 3 leads – Divorces, evictions and Pre-foreclosure flags: All new HOA/COA liens, county & state tax defaults and liens, evictions and various court judgments (such as for code violations).

And my tech team sources all of this data directly from the court records and never from public notices. So you'll be the first to know about every potential off-market deal in your county.

Visit our website for a tour of the software and even a free sample of local leads to whet your appetite.

www.lirankoren.com

2) We also offer all-inclusive hands-on coaching for wholesalers, cash investors, agents and auction bidders. This isn't some motivational pep talk, but real time coaching on specific deals you're working on now. We'll go into the nuts and bolts of setting up your sales infrastructure, evaluating every minute aspect of your deals, negotiating with homeowners & estate reps and securing financing or cash end buyers.

We guide you through every step of the process, doublechecking your math and due diligence along the way, until you're dominating

THE ULTIMATE GUIDE TO WHOLESALING

your local marketplace. The coaching bundle also includes a free year subscription to all the leads in your local market.

You can take a free preview tour of the course here to better see how we can help.

3) Don't have the time to build your own system from scratch and want to make the real dream of passive income a reality? Led by me personally and staffed by agents I've carefully trained, my full-service property management and investment acquisition company is your one-stop shop for building your portfolio and extracting maximum value from it while minimizing your stress and time investment.

Visit Luxury Property Care, LLC for a free consultation of what we can do for you in your local market.

www.luxurypropertycare.com

In any case, I'd love to hear your questions, complaints or suggestions for more topics to add in a second edition of this book. I'm always watching the reviews on Amazon to see how I can add more value. Any feedback you provide will be greatly appreciated.

About the Author

Liran Koren is an active high-volume investor in Florida and Co-Founder of Luxury Property Care.

He enjoys a good CrossFit workout or traveling anywhere new just as much as crunching data.

He also provides in-depth coaching and custom web scrapers through his educational venture at: www.lirankoren.com.

You can also hire his property management and investor acquisitions services directly at www.luxurypropertycare.com

Made in the USA
Coppell, TX
06 January 2023

10597054R00089